You've Really Got Me, God!

A Young Person's Search
for God's Will

Alan Porter

BAKER BOOK HOUSE
Grand Rapids, Michigan

ISBN: 0-8010-7019-8

Second printing, June 1978

Printed in the United States of America

p.5
1.45

To three fine Christian young men,
without whose experiences
this book could never have been written.
—Their Dad.

This is a logbook—the record of a spiritual journey. It is the story of Joel Stewart, of his growth from boyhood to manhood, of his experiences with his family, his friends, his Lord. It is the record of his searchings, his questions, his problems, his mistakes, his decisions. Most of all, it is the record of his maturing in Christ, his reaching out for guidance, his desire to find God's perfect will for his life. The story is written in the hopes that, by following Joel's struggles, other young people can find answers to their search for God's will, that they will be encouraged to commit their all to Christ, that they will share the joy of being completely His.

A.P.

CONTENTS

1
Senior Year in High School

Hello, God.

That's a funny way to start this.

But "Dear God" would make this sound like a prayer—which it isn't.

And just "God" might be disrespectful—which it also isn't.

So, Hello, God.

I'm going to keep a journal, like Pastor Rob suggested in youth meeting tonight.

Just some place I can write down my ideas about You.

And talk to You about my problems.

I don't know how this is going to turn out.

Like, here's this notebook, full of blank pages.

What's going to be written on them?

I get excited thinking about that.

Only You know what they will contain.

And that's what I'm going to find out, piecemeal.

You've really got me, God!

How can I find Your plan?

What shall I write tonight, God?

Maybe I'd better tell You about me, though You know it already.

I'm Joel Stewart.

I'm 17½—a senior at P.H.S.

I've a Mom, a Dad, two brothers (John and Jim), two cats, and a dog, Teddy.

I'm in the band (cornet) and run track (I'm out temporarily with a cracked toe).

9

I'm a baritone in youth choir at church.

So much for me.

Now, about me-and-You, which is what this journal is for.

How long have I known about You, God?

Forever, I think.

No, not really—only I never remember not hearing about You.

Even my earliest memories are of You . . . the hymns on the record-player as Mom tucked me in . . . Dad talking to You, standing there by my bed.

How long have I loved You?

Ever since that night (I was about five) when, after I'd heard a sermon on Your love, I called Dad and told him I wanted to love You.

We kneeled together by my bed and, in my childish way, I gave my heart to You.

Now I wonder, do I *really* know You, God?

That's what Pastor Rob asked us tonight.

He said You hold the key to our lives, You'll guide us in life's big decisions—if we'll let You.

That means trusting ourselves—all that we are and can be—to You.

That's why I'm starting this journal.

I want to think about You, write my thoughts to You, talk things over with You here.

I want to find Your plan for me: what I should do, what I should be.

Maybe by talking on paper like this, You can show me Your way.

Will You, God?

I really want to know.

God, this is Your dignified senior speaking.
"Dignified"—hardly!
"Senior"—to what?
Merely the oldest and the biggest in school—and nearest to being grown up.
Which is a little scary at times.
Because the more grown up a guy gets, the bigger the decisions he has to make.
I've found that out already.
So we'll have a lot to talk over, God, You and me, in this journal.
Like I've said, I want Your will for my life.
Only, what *is* Your will?
You've really got me, God!
I'm waiting . . .

I've got a little empty feeling today, God.
Funny—I didn't think I would have.
John left this morning, to go to college.
The first break in the family circle.
Of course, he's been gone before, but this time it's different.
When he comes home, he'll be changed—more grown up, probably, with different interests and friends.
Things won't ever be quite the same again.
You know, I'm really going to miss him.
That's a surprise!

Hey, God, I got a job!

Of course, You know already, but I'm writing it to see how it looks: I've got a job!

A *real* job, God, not just mickey-mouse paper-boy or leaf-raker jobs.

In the newspaper office!

I can hardly believe it.

It started by my writing up Little League games last summer, as a favor for Mr. Evens.

The items were noticed by the sports editor, and they must have been all right, because today he phones me.

"Stewart," he says, "we need a sports assistant to cover high school football this fall. Are you interested?"

I'm so surprised I can hardly answer.

"Sure," I say, "I'd like to very much."

"OK," he says, "You can start Friday night on the home game, and we'll see that you cover the away ones too. And, Joel," he adds, "if this works out, you can cover county games as well. Do you have a car to use?"

I assure him I do and he says, "Great, come in tomorrow and we'll talk about pay."

So I'm in, really in.

Isn't that great, God?

Work I really like—great experience, too!

Plus extra money, for all sorts of things.

Maybe it will even open into full-time journalism.

Who knows, God?

You do.

God, how do I tell a grown-up he's wrong?

Like my chemistry teacher, God—he's a really neat
guy, about twenty-two, just out of college, in his
first teaching job.

I know he's trying.

But, God, he doesn't know his chemistry, that's what!

Of course, I don't know that much myself, or else I
wouldn't be taking it.

But I do know when a formula's wrong on the board.

And his are wrong half the time.

Some guys don't realize this, and they're learning the
stuff wrong.

What do I do?

Send him an anonymous note: "Check your formulas:
the Master Chemist is watching"?

Say, "Pardon me, Mr. Grayson, but your formulas are
wrong"?

Raise a question, "I don't understand this formula;
could you check it out for me?"

Maybe I should just mind my own business.

Me, I can study it out myself, from the text.

But what about the other guys, God?

Perhaps I can help them, studying with them.

Perhaps Grayson will wise up and check what he
writes on the board.

Couldn't You give him just a little push in that direction, please?

About this college business, God—we're really rolling.

After I'd decided on college instead of training in
trades, after I'd narrowed down the possibilities, I

13

wrote to the three we'd talked about, You-and-I:
State (it's got a great marching band), Woodrow
(journalism department), Stoddard (band and track,
plus a Christian emphasis too).
All three answered, sending application blanks, which
I sweated over.
They want everything but your fingerprints and a
blood sample, don't they?
So I've sent in the applications ($10 each).
And I'm waiting.
I don't know how to pray about this.
I'm not pushing any one of the three.
But I am asking You to block the doors of those I
shouldn't attend.
Or else make one much more appealing than the rest.
Or else give me an inner feeling about one.
How about it, God?
Will You?

Wednesday, November 4th

God, I want to share something.
Something I'm trying to make my family think I really
don't care about.
I got a letter today, a commendation from the National
Merit Scholarship tests I took two months ago.
Inside, I'm happy, pleased, proud—very humble, too.
Thank You, God, for giving me a good mind and
helping me use it.
This letter will help me get into "the college of my
choice," the counselor says: it's already been sent
to my three choices.
Outside, I shrug and say, "Oh, it's nothing."
I squirm when Dad says, "Great, Son," and slaps me
on the back, when Mom looks at me happily.
What's wrong with me, both to want and resent praise?

Nothing, I hope.

It's just that I can't show outside what I really feel inside.

I know You understand, God.

What do You know, God?

Buzz and Cathy are getting married tomorrow, at the church, only their families there.

No waiting till they graduate, no big wedding, no nothing.

You know why, don't You?

They've got to get married, that's why.

God, that knocks the wind out of me.

Like, Buzz is only eighteen and Cathy seventeen; they haven't even finished school!

Buzz wants to go to college, but how can he, with a baby coming in July?

I can't imagine what it will be like for them—trying to go to school, be parents, keep a job, all at the same time.

Buzz won't have any time for fun things, like band, sports, horsing around with the guys.

He'll just have to study, work, take care of Cathy and the baby.

He'll just have to grow up all at once.

I know he'll manage, God; he's really a great guy.

And he truly loves Cathy, too—this is no ''one-night affair.''

What happened, God?

They've always been pretty special, active in church, loving You.

Did they just forget Your standards for them?

Did they want each other too badly to wait?

Were they tempted just a little too far?
Now here they are, stuck into being a family already.
They'll really try to make a go of it, I know they will.
But it won't be easy.
Is that the price they have to pay?
Help them, God—they'll need You.
And help me and my brothers never to get into their
    predicament.
It can't be much fun.

Friday, January 1st

Happy New Year, God!
Is it New Year's morning? or New Year's Eve "hung
    over"?
I wouldn't know; I haven't been to bed yet.
Two reasons for writing, God.
One: to start the New Year right, of course!
The other: more serious.
God, I can hardly believe what's happened: it sends
    cold, chilly ripples down my spine.
We all went together to watchnight service at the
    church, as usual.
Just about midnight, when we were all praying silently,
    the organ rolling in the background, we heard si-
    rens shrieking by outside.
We didn't pay much attention, though I did notice
    Pastor Rob was called out quietly.
At 12, the factory whistle blew and the church bells
    rang, and we all started yelling "Happy New Year!"
It was really exciting, God, a whole new year coming
    in!
Then Pastor Rob came back, looking strained, and he
    asked Sally Stratton and her cousin June to go into
    his office with him.
And he had to tell them the tragic news.

But I'm getting ahead of myself.

We guys pile out of church and into the old blue Ford, Dad having said we could stay out till 1.

And we drive down Main Street with the gang.

Only at Ninth Street, there are flashing red lights—two fire trucks, with a police car directing traffic around something.

Which we see in a moment are two badly smashed cars, right at the intersection.

We gape as we drive past, of course, and there—O dear God, I wish I hadn't looked!—I can't get it out of my mind—is a woman hanging halfway out of one car, her head smashed against the street, and a man humped over the steering wheel, which is jammed back into him.

They're dead, God, dead.

The ambulance men are just standing there, nothing they can do, and the firemen are chopping away at the car and washing gasoline down the drain.

And those two people are dead.

God, I never saw death before; I don't like what I saw.

What is especially awful is—they're Sally's parents, both of them.

How horrible!

And right as the new year begins—well, almost.

They were so happy together, that family.

What will Sally do?

Of course, her married brother, Henry, and her sister, Marilyn—You know, the one that works at Breton's—they'll be with her.

Why did it happen, God?

Did it have to happen?

Was that Your plan?

Or did someone mess up Your plan?

I'm so full of questions.

After seeing the accident, we drive to Willie's for a coke.

But it doesn't taste good, and the fun is gone.

So we come on home.

Mom and Dad are still up, so we all pray for Sally.

Then they turn in, and we guys talk a while, not wanting to be alone with our thoughts.

Finally we drift off to our separate rooms.

John's and Jim's lights are off; I guess they're sleeping, or trying to.

I should be trying also, God—but the sight and shock keep sweeping through my mind.

So that's why I've been writing.

I feel better now I've got it down.

Please help me get to sleep, God.

Please help Sally.

Good night.

Sunday, January 24th

Happy Birthday to me, God!

I'm eighteen today, an "adult."

I can sign papers, get any job, even get married without Dad's permission in some states (ha, ha).

I can also vote.

Pretty cool, eh?

But it really isn't all that big a deal.

(See, there I'm liking and not liking something at the same time, again!)

Mom and Dad gave me track shoes, a sports magazine subscription, and several buffalo nickels for my coin collection.

There was also a huge, suspiciously light-weight box for me to open.

Like, box inside box, inside box—four of them.

And inside the last one, a note: "Congratulations on being eighteen! From now on, when you're out at night, we'll not wait up for you. We'll leave the light

on, but go to bed. If you feel like talking when you
   get in, just knock at our door and we'll chat. Love, .
   Mom and Dad.''
How about that?
Like, that shows they trust me, they believe their love
   and training and prayers have paid off.
Let me never betray their trust, God.
Help me make them proud of me.
I want You to be proud of me, too.

Wednesday, February 17th

I think things are shaping up, God—about college, that
   is.
I've heard from all three schools: ''We'll have you, if
   you'll come.''
That's confusing.
But I'm feeling more of an inclination to one school
   than to the others.
Is this of You?
The phone rings today, and it's for me, the track coach
   at Stoddard.
Oh, I know it's a P.R. gimmick, but it does make me
   feel pretty good, his inviting me to run track for him.
Besides, there's a scholarship involved, which I can
   shoot for.
More and more, Stoddard comes to mind.
Is this the way You're leading?
I wish You'd drop a note down from heaven, with
   directions, or send me a brilliant dream.
But You don't work that way, do You?
OK, then, I've got this growing feeling about Stoddard,
   that ''This is it.''
Am I wrong, God?
Is this Your inner voice, saying, ''This is the way, walk
   ye in it''?

19

I think that's what it is.
So I think I'll accept Stoddard.
Please, even yet, stop me if I'm wrong.

Sunday, March 14th

Hello again, God.
I was reading back in the journal tonight, and I noticed
    something missing.
I haven't said anything about girls.
This year I haven't been interested in anyone special.
(Of course, I'm busy with my job—did I tell You I'm
    covering baseball now?)
Mostly, I just run around with the gang from church.
I did meet one girl—her name was Leona—at a youth
    rally.
And when I went to Farleyville (where she lives) to
    cover a game, we had a date.
But that romance never got off the ground.
I guess if I'd really been interested, I'd have pushed it.
Am I normal, God?
Most of the guys think there's nothing but girls: they
    brag what lady-killers they are, how much they
    "make out."
I don't want that kind of "love."
Mom says someday there'll be a special girl for me.
I hope so.
But right now, I don't care very much.

Wednesday, April 15th

Oh, God, I'm so disappointed.
I'd like to crawl under my bed, and stay there till it's
    over.
What's over?

20

Music contest, that's what.

Like, You know how hard I've been working on my solo for competition, Lord—hours and hours of practice, getting fingering just right, toughening up my lip?

I've memorized the whole thing, too, and worked on timing, phrasing, tone.

So what happens?

Suddenly it's all down the drain, God—kaput, no good.

When I went in to band today, God, I knew something was wrong.

Mr. Jackson comes right over to me, not smiling as usual.

In fact, he's sort of embarrassed and awkward, not like a teacher at all.

I like Mr. Jackson, God—he's really a great guy, helping me with cornet and all.

Well, anyway, he comes right out with it (he's always direct).

"Joel," he says, "I don't know how to put this, but—I've made a terrible mistake."

"What about?" I ask, icy fingers clutching at my heart.

"Well," he says, "about that piece you've been working up . . ."

"Yep," I say, remembering the "blood, sweat, and tears" I've put into it.

"Well," says he, "I hate to say this, but that piece isn't on the schedule for this year."

That takes a few seconds to sink in, then POW! it hits me.

If it isn't on the list, I can't play it at the contest.

Mr. Jackson goes on, "I don't know how I could have made that mistake; it's on last year's list, but not this."

He adds, pleading-like, so I know it makes him sick,

"Sometimes a piece is on two years in a row, you
  know."
Well, if he's sick, how does he think I feel?
Like wishy-washy, sick to my stomach, literally.
Just two days to contest, Lord—what do I do?
I can't bluff and play this piece anyway: they'd throw
  me out after three measures.
I can't work up another at this late date.
I can't complain: that would only do Mr. Jackson in,
  and it was, after all, an honest mistake.
Why did it have to happen?
And to me, my last chance at state contest?

Thursday, April 16th

Well, I quit moping, God.
I said, "Stewart, don't cry over spilt milk."
I said, "You're still in the brass cornet quartet, so give
  that everything you've got."
Which we did, and we've practiced, and I think we're
  really ready to produce.
The hurt will be there for a while.
But hurting is part of growing up, isn't it?
Maybe I've grown up a little through this experience.
Tell You one thing, though, God.
If ever I'm a band teacher (which I won't be) and if ever
  I assign a piece for contest, I'll be sure it's on the list
  before I use it.

Thursday, May 13th

Just one more week, God!
Then I'll be a P.H.S. alumnus!
Back when I was little, I thought things always would
  go on the same.

22

I'd always be in school, running around with the guys,
  playing ball, being home.
Now I know things change.
Here I am nearly at the end of this road.
And it isn't as exciting as I thought it'd be.
Oh, in some ways it is: the beginning of a new world,
  in college.
But it's also the end of an old, comfortable, familiar
  one, here.
That's kind of scary.
Am I ready to leave home?
To work to help put myself through college?
To face life's big decisions?
Will I someday look back on this year as my last
  carefree time in life?
There's no going back, is there, God?

Friday, May 21st

They're over, God, my high school days.
Rah! rah! for "good ole" P.H.S.!
Graduation was something else again.
They had a brainstorm: let's hold it outdoors, in the
  stadium.
OK, if you can count on the weather—which you can't
  always.
So yesterday dawns bright and blue—good.
So we go to the stadium about 6:30, decked out in blue
  caps-and-gowns.
And we're lined up ready to march in.
When WHEEEEEEE, a fierce wind rips out of the north,
  out of nowhere.
It was really funny—hats flying everywhere, programs
  swirling like huge snowflakes, guys running, trip-
  ping over their robes—we started laughing so hard
  we could hardly stop.

23

And cold! The temperature must have dropped twenty
   degrees.
So we sit there, shivering, hanging onto our caps,
   trying not to listen to the speaker drone on.
(You know, the same old line, " . . . setting sail on the
   sea of life . . . ")
Then it's over, and we're thumping each other, cheer-
   ing.
Then there's the all-night Senior party, which Mom
   and Dad said I could decide about going to.
Which I do, there being lots of good fun and breakfast
   at 3:30.
So about 4 I get home and tumble into bed.
Is it the end of the beginning?
The beginning of the end?
Or what?

Monday, June 7th

Vacation time, God!
But not a time to loaf.
I've got two jobs this summer—isn't that great?
I'm half-time on the newspaper staff, lots of sports
   writing to do.
And they've asked me to coach a Little League team.
Which I'll do gladly, remembering how much fun I
   had in Little League.
Help me to be a good coach, God.
The kind the little guys can look up to, and love, and
   admire.
Help me to help them grow.

Tuesday, August 17th

Wouldn't You know it, God?

24

Now, just now, when I'm about to leave for college, I
  meet a really neat girl, Tammy.
Her folks moved here from Memphis last month;
  they're coming to our church.
She's quiet, pretty, brunette—and very, very sweet.
We've had coke dates after choir, and bowled, and
  played minature golf.
Things look good—only now I've got to leave.
Just my luck!
Of course, I'll be home Thanksgiving.
And Tammy has promised to write.
So maybe we can keep it going.
You can bet I'll try, anyway!

2
Freshman Year in College

It's late, God, I know.
But I have to write to You tonight, this last night before I
leave home.
In the quietness, I look around the familiar room.
There's the map on the wall, the spider web in the
corner of the ceiling, the drapes stained by the
ketchup John threw at me once, the games in the
bookcase.
I've put away my high school stuff.
I've stored my coins in the safe deposit box.
I've given my goldfish to Jim.
I think I have everything done.
Everything except saying Goodbye to the old life.
And Hello to the new.
I feel confused, God.
I want to go—and I don't want to.
I'm excited—and scared.
I want to be on my own—and I need assurance from
home.
What courses will I take?
Who will I meet?
What career will I prepare for?
How can I make all the decisions that have to be
made?
Lord, if You weren't going with me, I'd back out now!

Here I am, God, twenty-four hours later and 600 miles
    away.
In my new home, my dorm room at Stoddard.
I really hated to see Dad and Mom drive away.
And Jim—poor guy, no brothers at home to bother him
    any more.
Does he miss us now that we're gone?
Or is he glad, because he has the old blue Ford to
    himself?
My roommate's a pretty good guy—a football player,
    from Michigan.
But he likes the window open; I don't.
I like to stay up late; he doesn't.
How do they match up roommates, God, by pulling
    names out of a goldfish bowl?
Hope we get along OK.
Oh, well, I'll make friends.
I hope.
You'll stick pretty close, won't you, God?
I'm going to need You a lot these next few days.

It's registration day, God.
Which means I must "pick and choose."
What do I take?
Like, I'll knock off the required subjects, of course.
But choosing sections? teachers? hours?
How do I know what's best?
Oh, the upperclassmen have dished out plenty of free
    advice: "That course's easy; you'll psych it out,"
    and "Stay away from Old Fuddy; his classes are a
    drag."

I've drawn up a tentative schedule, like they showed
    us in orientation yesterday.
Now I've got an appointment with Dr. Mason, my
    advisor.
Look, God, keep me going in Your path, will You?
Even though I don't know where I'm going right now,
    help me get there!
Thanks, God.

Thursday, September 16th

Help, God, I'm sinking!
I'm in over my head—in philosophy, no less.
Like, I probably shouldn't have signed into it yet.
But Dr. Mason thought it might be OK for me.
So, eager beaver, I sign up and buy me the textbook—a
    $9 book, even.
So I sit in class and hear, "cognition," "epistemol-
    ogy," "teleology" . . .
My head's spinning: I don't have a ghost of an idea
    what it's all about.
What'll I do, God?

Friday, September 17th

Well, it was easy enough, God.
Like, I go see Dr. Mason and drop the course.
Just like that.
I've substituted math: I'm much more at home in that.
I'll face philosophy later.
When I feel ready for it.

Sunday, September 26th

Two-and-a-half weeks, God.
And not one line from Tammy!
I've sent her two cards (pictures of campus) and a note, too.
You'd think she'd answer.
Why doesn't she, God?
She promised she would.

Sunday, October 3rd

Still no note from Tammy, God.
Do you suppose she's lost my address?
No, I guess not; it's been on all the mail I've sent her.
Maybe she's just busy?
I hope that's all.

Friday, October 8th

Hey, thanks, God!
There it was in the mailbox today, pert as You please—a letter from Tammy.
On flowered stationery (I hope the guys didn't see it), smelling pretty.
Of course, I was dying to read it.
But I was on my way to class, and who can read a letter when he's trying to write a compostion?
So I peeked at it; then came to my room after class to read it.
It was kinda short, God.
But kinda sweet, too—I think.
It did seem a bit impersonal.
Maybe it's hard for Tammy to put her thoughts down on paper.

Writing comes naturally to me.
But some people find it hard.
So I'm satisfied, God.
I think I'll answer it tonight.
Or would that look too eager?

Hey, God, I'm going out for track!
When I got here, see, I met Coach Svenson
—remember, he phoned me last February?
He's really neat, God, a tall, blond Swede with a super
build.
Somehow, he makes me feel as if I'm wanted—little
old amateur me.
Now that I'm here, I see the competition I'll be up
against.
I'm realizing I'm not such a hot runner.
But Coachie (he likes to be called that) is real en-
couraging.
"Not bad," he says, after I've run my heart out in a
sprint. "Of course, we'll have to work on that knee
action," and "Why don't you hold your elbows
back more?" and "Watch your breathing," and
"We'll make champs of you all yet. Now get out
there and *run!*"
And, boy, do we run!
We run for ourselves, our own satisfaction—and for
him because he believes in us.
If/when I'm ever a track coach (which I don't plan to
be), I'll be like him.
Run, guys, run!

Monday, November 1st

All these books, library, term papers, exams, God!

31

And me, I aced out in high school, hardly ever cracking a book outside of school.

So, now the Big Awakening.

Like, mid-terms coming up . . . two tests and a paper between now and Thursday!

What comes first?

My history paper? studying for math? cramming for Bible?

("Cramming for Bible"—that's a farce: I figured I knew my Bible, what with a Christian home, and church activities and all. But now I'm finding out all I don't know. Is that what I came to college for?)

Well, sitting here isn't getting it done.

I've got to work out a schedule, and stick to it.

Look out, Stoddard: here comes "The Scholar."

I only hope he makes it through!

Monday, November 8th

God, what is the matter with Tammy?

Why doesn't she write?

Just a measly little line, a postcard—anything.

She promised, God.

Didn't she mean it?

Here it's a whole month since her note; nine weeks into the semester!

About two months ago, I sent her an addressed, stamped envelope.

Like a big fat hint: Why don't you write?

Was she mad about it, God?

Did she take it as a joke?

I hoped she'd at least send it back; but nothing.

I've written several times: personal, but not too personal, friendly, but not too friendly.

It's hard to write to a girl: they try to read between the lines.

Sometimes that scares me.

I try reading too, before I mail the letters, to see what's there.

Maybe Tammy read something she didn't like?

Or didn't find something she was hoping to?

What is it, God?

It's good Thanksgiving's coming up.

Two weeks from Wednesday, I'm home.

Guess I'll find out what's what then.

(But I'm almost afraid to.)

Friday, November 26th

Well, I found out, all right, God.

She's just not interested in me. Period.

There, I had to write it down.

It's hard to write; it's even harder to accept.

I get home late Wednesday, after the long drive from Stoddard.

And after supper, we all go to the church Thanksgiving service.

Tammy's there—by herself, not with another guy, which is a relief.

After service, I ask to take her home, and she says, "Sure!"

So we stop at Willie's, as usual, and see the rest of the old gang.

And she's friendly and all that.

Before we get to her house, I stop the car.

"Look," I say, "I've been hoping you'd write."

She shrugs, "I'm not very good at letters."

"Well, I don't care what you write, just as long as you do. I've just kept hoping and hoping."

She's nice about it, God—too nice.

"Thanks for the thought," she says, "but I don't think I'll be writing at all."

33

"Oh?" I ask. "Someone else?"

"No, nobody else," she says. "Look, I like you a lot and all that. But I don't think we'd better keep in touch."

"Why?" I blunder on, dumbly.

"Because I like you, but that's all."

"That's all?" I can't turn myself off.

"Yes, I enjoy talking and dating, but you have your college career and I have my job, and I don't think we're supposed to keep this thing going."

"In other words, you don't like me," I accuse.

"Can't you understand?" she asks impatiently. "I just said I like you, but that's all, as far as I'm concerned."

"You mean, you're not interested any more?" I go on.

"Well, if you put it that way, Yes," she says, piling out of the car. "Thanks for the coke. Good night."

That was that.

What a letdown, God!

Thursday, December 9th

It's You-and-me again, God.

Like, the old question: What do You want me to do?

It's Mission Emphasis Week, see, with some really good speakers on campus.

Like this morning's speaker: not bombastic (neat word, eh?) or especially dynamic.

Just a quiet-spoken, logical, sincere man.

I felt drawn to his message about Your will.

Was I drawn to him? or to You?

No, I don't have an urge to sprint to the nearest mission board and sign up.

But are missions for me?

I've got a long road ahead: still seven semesters of college.

But I need direction, God.
I'll consider missions if You want me to.
Lead me, please.

It was a really neat Christmas, God!
Home again, all three of us guys together, almost like
   the old days (after the strangeness wore off).
The place looked smaller (it had at Thanksgiving, too),
   but my room was the same as always (except that
   cobweb was gone).
Poor Mom, when she opened my "Christmas pre-
   sent," that huge box, and found it full of laundry to
   be done—You should have seen her face!
But she sure had been busy getting ready for us—
Fruit cake, pecan pie, tollhouse cookies, turkey—the
   works.
Everything was so familiar.
The old blue Ford—we about wore out—driving
   around like always.
Nothing to spoil it, not even Tammy (she went back to
   Memphis for Christmas).
Just perfect, God, just perfect.
And now I'm back, and this seems just right, too.
I really feel at home here now.
Probably it's because I'm where You want me to be.
It's a good feeling.

Exams, God, ugh!
They loom like monsters, leering at me.
I feel like David going out to meet Goliath, or Tom
   Thumb facing the cat.

Please help me, God.
I've done my best: I've studied hard.
Help me do my best now, for my own self-confidence.
And for You.

Wednesday, February 9th

Meet the new sportswriter for the *Stoddard Standard*,
   God!
Yep, little ole me, lowly "frosh" and all!
There's this notice on the bulletin, "Sportswriter
   wanted."
So I check into it.
They peruse my credentials, have me peck out a hasty
   column, look at it critically.
"You're on," they say. "No pay, no expense account,
   just hard work."
Frankly, I don't think they had any other applicants!
Who cares?
Someday I'll be famous, and give them credit for my
   experience.
Would you believe?

Friday, February 18th

Here's a secret, God.
I got my grades today: 1 "A" (Freshman Comp) and 3
   "B"'s last semester.
Not bad—for a greenhorn from Colorado!
I wish I had someone to show them to.
But then I wouldn't, because it would seem like brag-
   ging.
(That's me: proud and embarrassed at the same time.)
I made the Dean's list, which is something.

If I need good grades (to get into grad school), these
   will help.
Thanks for helping me, God.

What a work-out, God!
Coachie is really putting us through the paces.
Like, this indoor track meet is coming up, and it's 5
   a.m. runs, daily exercises, workouts after classes,
   run, run, run.
I have muscles I never dreamed of—and they all ache.
But I'm tightening up and getting into good shape,
   God.
Maybe You'll need a guy in good shape for some
   special work.
OK, I'll be ready!

Easter today, God.
The day to remember Your Son's resurrection.
Thanks for today's beauty: the warm sunshine, the
   alive feeling in the air, new leaves, robins.
Thanks for Christ in my heart, living proof of His resur-
   rection.
It's funny—I'm homesick today, the first time I've
   really been homesick since coming to college.
It seemed wise, at the time, not to go home for Easter,
   what with bus fare, track practice, studies and all.
I'm thinking of our church, the choir, the music, my
   friends—and my folks.
I wish I were there, but I'm not.
God, did You feel lonely like this when Your Son went
   away?
Then You understand.

I haven't dated yet this year, God, but I want to for the spring concert.

There's a cute redhead from Iowa in my history class: I think she likes me.

And there's Sue, who works in the cafeteria: she knows I like tomatoes, so she tosses an extra piece into my salad bowl.

I don't want to get stuck on anyone (I remember Tammy).

But just a fun date.

Who shall I ask?

I think Sue.

OK, God?

I'm hurting God, really hurting.

Just when I was going to ask Sue to the concert, I hurt my knee in track.

Hurt it read bad, too—skinned, bleeding, tendons slightly torn.

So here I am, hobbling around on crutches.

I'm hurt inside, too.

Coachie was counting on me for the tri-college meet the end of the month.

Now I guess I'm out.

What a letdown!

Also, how can a guy date on crutches?

I couldn't even make it to Sue's dorm to pick her up.

To say nothing of getting up into the balcony (which are the only seats I could afford) on crutches.

Help me have some more chances to run.

Give me another chance at Sue, will You?

Registration again, God!
Fall semester coming up . . .
Dr. Mason is going to ask what I'd like to major in.
And I don't know.
Can't major in journalism here . . . how about English?
Sociology? Psychology?
Social work? (So I can work with people)?
I think my interests are narrowing, but I don't want to
    declare yet.
Not until I'm surer of Your plan.
"Guide me, O thou great Jehovah."
I need Your thoughts.

Monday, May 8th

I'm trying, God, really trying!
To get a job at home for the summer.
I've written to (1) the post office, (2) the office furniture
    factory, (3) Breton's department store, even (4) the
    sausage plant (oink).
Now I'll have to wait and see what opens up.
I hope *something* does.

Friday, June 2nd

The semester's over, God.
Where did my freshman year go?
Tomorrow I head for home; everything's packed and
    ready.
But what am I going home *to*?
No job yet, God—and nothing else I can think of to do.
What do You have for me?

Well, God, what *do* You have for me?

Anything?

Like the post office: they've a list of applicants a mile long.

And the furniture factory: slow-down of orders, no summer work.

And Breton's: sorry, no openings right now.

Even the sausage factory: we'll call you if anything opens up.

So what do I do?

Funny, my two old jobs from last summer are available—You know, the coaching for Little League and the part-time work at the newspaper.

But I wanted a full-time, man-sized job.

Of course, "a bird in the hand," I suppose.

I *do* have those two options.

Should I take them, Lord?

I guess I should.

Time on my hands, God!

And I don't like it.

The newspaper and coaching are fine—but I have most of the daytimes free.

Can you find me something to do then?

Look, God, I didn't expect that answer.

After last year's grind at the books—how come I'm back at it again?

In the *summer*, no less?

Like there I am, grumbling about nothing to do.

And Dad tosses a catalog from the junior college at me.

"Quit complaining and see what you can find here for diversion," he says. "Maybe you could get a jump ahead in your college work."

Well, I don't like the idea much, but I do look at the catalog.

And here are these two courses, see, basic ones, both transferable—English lit and economics.

So I snoop around and find out about 'em, and presto!

Here I am, registered for the two courses . . . plus the newspaper . . . plus the Little League.

How will I get everything done?

Thursday, July 6th

Things are looking up, God.

Like, I bumped into this girl I used to see around high school.

Only she was a sophomore when I was a senior.

And no senior in his right mind ever looks at sophomores.

Her name is Cheryl, and she's about up to my shoulder, with short blonde hair.

Pretty as a picture.

She's singing in our church youth choir: maybe I should join it for the summer?

Think I will!

Monday, July 24th

Hmmm, not bad, God.

Cheryl's real fun: I've dated her here and there this month.
She even comes out and cheers my Little League team!
She's really cute—and I think she likes me, God.
She's asked me to dinner Sunday.
That's a good sign, isn't it, God?

Tuesday, August 22nd

What happens now, God?
Just as things are getting good with Cheryl, whoosh, I'm off to college again.
We've been going out for seven weeks now, pretty steady.
She hasn't accepted any other dates, though I know she's been asked.
We have a lot in common—love of sports, cherry cokes, even You.

Wednesday, August 30th

Well, I asked her, God.
She said she'd be my girlfriend; she even said she'd write to me.
I didn't ask her not to date anyone else: that wouldn't be fair, me being away and all.
But if she's for me and I'm for her, she won't go out, will she?
Well, I can't worry about that.
I've marked on the calendar the weekend of October 28th-29th.
That's when I'll go home for a few days with Cheryl.

Like, nine weeks, sixty-three days . . . I'll count them
   down, You be sure!
It's been a good summer, God.
Hasn't it?

3
Sophomore Year in College

Thursday, September 8th

Wise fool, God—that's me!
(That's a paradox: see, I remember my literary terms!)
Why do I say so?
Because that's what "sophomore" means—see Webster!
It just fits, God, perfectly.
Sometimes I'm wise, learning a lot.
Sometimes I'm a fool, dumb as a dodo.
Well, at least I'm aware of the paradox.
And working to change it.
Like, I'm really digging into this "getting wisdom" bit . . .
And not forgetting the other part: " . . . with all thy getting, get understanding."
Make me wise.
Make me understanding, I pray, God.

Tuesday, September 13th

Ready for this lap, God!
Crouched on the blocks, every muscle quivering . . . taking deep breaths . . . tensing up . . . ready for the starting gun.
How's that for a metaphor of life, God?
OK, here are my courses: sociology, natural science, Bible doctrine, French (ooh, la, la!).
Ready, set—bang!—I'm off, for my second year at Stoddard!

I need a job, God.

Not a very big one—my studies are very demanding
   this year.

But a part-time one, maybe one day a week?

Just for a little spending money.

Got any ideas?

Hey, I just remembered the odd-job bulletin board!

How about that?

You answered my prayer by making me do something
   myself!

Right, God, here I go!

There it was, God.

Ready and waiting for me.

"Wanted: two college men to help with landscape
   work on Saturdays."

So I promptly phone the number listed, I go over for a
   short interview (Do I know which end of the rake to
   hold?).

And I'm on, starting this Saturday.

If it doesn't rain.

Thanks, God.

Good news today, God.

A letter from Cheryl, just like her own sweet self.

Only not as good as real, because I couldn't talk back,
   there and then.

Of course, I've answered it already.

But I sure wish we could go out tonight.

This long-distance business—it's not so hot, is it?
Well, only five weeks till October 28th . . . thirty-five
    days to go.

Saturday, October 1st

Love that job, God!
Outdoors these dreamy autumn days, blue haze in the
    sky, warm sunrays, burning leaves, crunchy grass
    underfoot . . .
My muscles get stronger, my head clears; it's what I
    need after the week's grind in the books.
I feel so close to You, working in Your world.
Love it, God!

Wednesday, October 12th

God, I made the track team!
The real team, not the second one!
And it's all due to Coachie—and You, of course.
Here I am struggling with the 440-yard sprint, and
    getting winded.
So Coachie switches me to the 110-yard dash.
Only then I can't get up and off the blocks fast enough.
So he tries the 220—which is *just right*.
(I feel like something out of Goldilocks and the Three
    Bears.)
Now he's really training me.
Like, the early morning workouts, chugging along the
    almost-deserted streets, watching the sun come up,
    purple, orange, gold in the east . . .
The wind on my face, crisp air in my lungs . . .
My knees chop-chopping rhythmically, my feet clop-
    clopping.

There are a couple of dogs who think I'm running for them, I guess.
At least, they join me at the corner of Tenth and Drew, sprinting along with me four blocks; a lean, red Irish setter and a small, pudgy terrier whose legs pump faster than mine, trying to keep up.
I get back, glowing inside, ready for a quick shower, breakfast.
Then, look out, world, here I come!
Know what I like best about those morning jogs, God?
The chance to be alone, to think, to talk with You.
We've had some great talks, haven't we?
What a great way to start the day!

Friday, October 21st

What gives, God?
A repeat of last year's disaster (with Tammy)?
Here it is, two weeks since Cheryl's last letter.
Did I imagine it, or was that one a little distant, disinterested even?
I've heard that "Absence makes the heart grow fonder."
I hope that's true.
I've also heard, "Absence makes the heart grow fonder—for someone else."
Is that what's happening?
God, I hope not.
If I weren't going home next weekend, I'd cut out now and go.
Just seven more days, and we can get it straightened out.
I hope.

What a wasted weekend, God.

What a dumb, wasted weekend.

It took all my time and strength; I'm so tired.

It took all my hard-earned cash from my landscape
    job; I'm broke.

For what, God?

For nothing, that's what.

Absolutely nothing.

I write Cheryl about our weekend, the one we've
    planned so long.

And she seems real happy, anticipating it like I am.

So I cut Friday classes (which I shouldn't have, since I
    missed a French test).

And I fly home (the bus would take too long).

I get there about 5 p.m. Friday, really excited.

I phone Cheryl about the football game, and she
    sounds great.

But she says, "Don't bother picking me up, Joel. I'll
    meet you there."

Which sounds funny.

But I'm so happy I overlook that.

Anyhow, I go to the stadium and get a general admis-
    sion ticket, like Cheryl suggested.

And I wait, watching for her.

Soon, there she comes, up the tier, cute as ever, her
    short, crisp blonde hair bobbing.

Me, I stand and wave frantically, like a kid who knows
    the answers in school.

Then I notice, two steps behind her—no, *with* her—is
    Pete Corbin.

I never liked Pete, God.

I like him even less now.

At first I don't realize he's with her; I think they've just
    happened to come in at the same time.

49

But he tags along as she comes up to where I am.

She sits down beside me, and he sits on the other side of her, like he belongs.

"Hi, Cheryl," I say, reaching for her hand.

(I want to kiss her, but don't dare right there in the stands.)

She says, "Hi Joel," flipping her hair in that tantalizing way that gets me.

She grins warmly, but doesn't move toward me.

All the time, there's Pete next to her glowering.

So we make small, unimportant talk, about how are things in the old home town and how are you doing in school—all the stupid things people talk about when they're dodging what they really want to say.

Finally she looks up brightly and says, "Oh, Joel, I guess you know Pete Corbin."

"Yeah," I grunt, and he nods brusquely.

She says, "I'm sorry I forgot to tell you I was coming to the game with Pete tonight."

Pete nods, belligerently, possessively.

Me, what can I say?

I swallow hard, to hide my disappointment.

"What do you mean, 'forgot'?" I choke out. "Look, Cheryl, I've come 600 miles to see you. Can't I at least see you after the game?"

She shoots a glance at Pete, like she's trying to get a signal.

"Not tonight, Joel," she says. "I'm going out with Pete."

And she winks at me.

Like, what does that wink mean?

That she's playing a game with Pete?

Or with me?

That she wants to go out with me but can't?

Or won't?

Man, do I feel let down.

Here I am, tired, nerved up, broke, sitting at a football
   game I don't even want to see, with the girl I've
   come to date sitting with that lug, Pete.

It doesn't make sense.

Well, Pete whispers something to her, and she smiles
   brightly at me.

"Joel, we really should go down and sit with the
   gang."

So I say right out, desperate-like, "But when can I see
   you, Cheryl? How about tomorrow afternoon?"

She thinks a minute, a long, long minute.

Then she perks up with, "OK, Joel. Pick me up at
   three."

Pete, he mutters something under his breath, and she
   says, "Shut up, Pete," and "How about it, Joel?"

Me, I'm ready to take any crumbs she offers, any
   crumbs at all.

So I say, "Fine; see you tomorrow."

And she and Pete disappear into the crowd.

I don't even watch them, to see whether they're "just
   friends" or maybe going together.

I'm not interested in the stupid game.

So I crawl down the stadium tier and go home.

I think Mom and Dad are surprised to see me back so
   early, but they don't pry.

So I flop into bed and zonk out.

Saturday afternoon, I pick Cheryl up and we drive
   around, just talking.

Saturday night I take her to the movies, and we end up
   at Willie's for coffee.

Everything seems good.

Sunday I take her to church, and her folks invite me
   over for dinner.

And things are good.

After dinner, we go out for a ride.

I can tell something's bothering her, real bad.

She says, "Joel, I've got to tell you something."

And she waits, for me to encourage her to go on, I guess.

But I don't say a thing.

This has got to come from her.

She starts again, "Joel, I know you're disapppointed about this weekend."

"So what's new?" I ask.

I guess I shouldn't have answered so sharply, but the frustration, the hurt, all sweep over me at once.

She glances over quickly, like she's trying to gauge my reactions.

Then she looks away, out the window.

"I suppose you've guessed," she says. "Pete and I are going steady."

Now, that's something I didn't expect.

A date or two, yes . . . but going steady?

Here, all the time I've been waiting, hoping—yes, Lord, even praying—she's been forgetting me.

She tells me a little about it, which I don't want to hear but have to.

Like, how lonesome she's been for me (I'll bet), and how she's missed having someone to run around with (you can say that again) and how Pete asked her out one night and she had a good time (yeah, man) and now he thinks she's his girl.

Well, suddenly I get mad.

Everything's mixed up together: love, hurt, anger.

I say right out, point blank, "Cheryl, do you love me?"

She's surprised, sort of taken aback, a little embarrassed.

I go on, blindly, "Or do you love Pete?"

She's very quiet.

I wonder if I've hurt her—I can't do that, God, no matter what she does to me.

I steal a glance at her, and she's sitting, sort of thinking.

"This is it," I say to myself. "She doesn't love me at all."

And she doesn't.

She finally says so, in a meek little voice, which gets to me.

I can read, loud and clear, what she is *really* saying, like "It was just a summer romance," and "It's over as far as I'm concerned," and "Pete's here and you aren't, so what do you expect?" and so on.

Well, we talk a little more, but the fizz is all gone.

So I drive her home and we say Goodbye.

Not "So long," or "Don't forget to write."

Just, Goodbye.

Period.

As she leaves, she smiles, a small, sadness-tinted smile.

Which makes me realize she knows I'm hurting inside.

And maybe she's feeling a little sorry for me.

Which she ought to.

I drive away and go home.

I pack up, check the airline, make a reservation, and take off, leaving my parents wondering and a little bewildered, I'm sure.

Only I can't talk about it to them.

Or to anyone, except You, God.

Here I am back, in my quiet dorm room.

Tired, empty, broke, drained.

No girl, no dreams, no hopes, no money.

What a wasted weekend, God.

What a dumb, wasted weekend.

Friday, November 25th

Haven't felt like writing, God.
I know You understand.

53

I'm all mixed up in my feelings.

What's wrong with me, God?

I want a girlfriend, but every time I reach out, I'm left
holding burst bubbles.

God, my spirits are really low tonight.

Sunday, November 27th

Got the answer, Lord!

Keeping busy—I think it's called "sublimation" in
psychology!

Classes . . . track . . . sports editing . . . landscape job
. . . I've plenty to do.

It does help.

I guess You're keeping busy, too, looking out for me.

Wednesday, November 30th

Pretty good timing, God.

My landscape job runs out last week, winter having
arrived.

And today I get a letter from Civil Service.

I'd forgotten to tell You—I took the tests some weeks
ago.

They always employ a bunch of college students at the
post office over the Christmas rush.

So I took the tests; passed them; and I'm on.

Starting a week from today.

First four hours a night; then eight, as Christmas gets
closer.

Thanks, God.

Give me strength, please.

Man, am I bushed, God!
Like, work all night, go to classes, try to study . . . what a life!
I get home from work about 5 a.m.
Tumble into bed for two, two and a half hours.
Up for 8 o'clock class—no breakfast, no shower, not enough sleep.
Stagger through classes, grab dinner, sack out from 1 till 4.
Study, eat supper, back to the P.O. for another round.
It's a nightmare, a real nightmare.
Only good thing, it won't last much longer.
And it does pay well!

Wednesday, December 28th

Home again, God, for Christmas.
I've slept around the clock these first three days; not surprising is it?
Such a nice feeling, though, being home Christmas.
It's where a guy belongs.
Especially since You're here too.
Our shared love for You—that's what makes Christmas so special.
Thank You for what Christmas means.

Friday, January 20th

Christian Vocations week, God.
All week long, a parade of speakers, some in "full-time" Christian work, others in "secular" vocations.

The message that has come through to me is, There is
   nothing "secular" in Your sight.
Is that true?
If so, I'm glad, because I've been struggling with that.
Somehow I've had the idea that only church-related
   occupations can be called "Christian" careers.
Now I see that no matter what I do, it can be dedicated
   to You.
OK, God, so what are my options?
(These are not in order of preference.)
   (1) Journalism
   (2) Social work of some sort (counseling? welfare?
      poverty programs?)
   (3) Peace Corps or Vista
   (4) Coaching/physical education
   (5) Forest ranger work
I could give You reasons for each area of interest, but
   You know those already.
Is this "bent" I feel toward some fields and away from
   others of You?
If so, "bend" me further, God.
Mold me into Your will.
This I ask, God—and I mean it.

Monday, January 30th

God, I've got a serious problem.
No, not girls again.
Remember when I had mono—I must have been about
   fourteen—and my neck glands were so swollen?
Well, they're swollen again, just a little infection, I
   guess.
What worries me is that in the swelling, there's a little
   hard lump.
Right under my chin, back toward my ear—there, feel
   it, God?

56

It's only little.
But I don't think it should be there.
What about it, God?
Can You make it go away?
Please do.

Saturday, February 8th

God, today I'm walking across campus and Steve
    zooms by on his new cycle, spins around, comes
    back.
"Hop on, " he says. "I'll take you to the gym."
Which is where I happen to be going.
He tosses me a helmet, which I put on, and look like a
    man from outer space.
I straddle the back seat, clutching Steve's middle, and
    whoosh! we're off.
Exhilaration, God—sheer exhilaration!—the whistling
    wind, the momentum, the almost-floating sensa-
    tion!
But you know that rutty road behind the gym?
You guessed it.
We zip along that road and there, smack dab in front of
    us, is a chuckhole big enough to get lost in.
Which Steve swerves to avoid, the motorcycle skid-
    ding, wheels spinning, careening suddenly, slither-
    ing along on one side.
Me, I go flying off—straight up then straight down,
    right on my tail bone!
I land so hard I bite my tongue and my head jolts like
    it's going to pop off.
I struggle up and stand, take a few steps—so I figure
    nothing's damaged permanently.
Except my dignity—and my back end.
Trouble is, God, I guess I had the helmet on the wrong
    end!

Kidding aside, thanks for keeping it from being worse.
I think I'll walk next time.

God, that lump's still there.
I was wishing You'd make it go away.
Maybe Your help will come some other way.
It's even a little bigger, Lord—oh, not as big as a golf ball, or even a marble.
About the size of one of Mom's beads, the big white ones she wears in summer.
What should I do about it?.
Tell Mom and Dad?
But I don't want to worry them.

It's worrying me, God.
I've got to tell somebody besides You.
Somebody human, I mean, somebody I can talk out loud about it to.
I think I had better tell my parents when I go home for spring break.
Do You mind, God?

Hey, God, this has been a great experience!
Coachie comes to me a few weeks ago (I guess I didn't write this).
"Stewart," he says, "I'm taking some track men on a short tour during spring break to some meets in Tennessee and Missouri. Think you'd like to go?"

Like to go?

Man, I jump at the chance.

Coachie grins, "OK, Joel. Work out in the 220 and
we'll show 'em Stoddard's 'greats'!"

So I work out—work my heart out—day after day.

OK, so we've been in four meets this week.

And guess what, God—I've got two medals.

Oh, not firsts—I'm not that good—but one second and
one third!

Not bad for a dumb jerk from P.H.S.

Surprising what a couple of years of real training can
do for a guy.

Mostly, it gives me self-confidence.

I can run—run well—well enough to pick up some
medals in stiff competition!

Oh, I'll never be a Jim Ryun . . . .

But I'm me, Joel Stewart.

Running with joy inside of me.

Monday, April 10th

It helps, God, it really helps.

That someone else knows about that lump.

See, after the track tour, I go home for 4 days.

I screw up my courage, finally, and tell Mom and Dad
about it.

They're great—they don't think I'm stupid for worrying.

They feel gently, and there, sure enough, is the lump,
right under their fingertips.

They're all for setting up an appointment with Dr.
Johnson at once.

But I persuade them to wait until summer.

So I've got a date with the Sawbones—for June 10th,
two months from today.

Please let the doctor say, "It's nothing."
Please, God.

Registration again, God—for my junior year!
Junior? Can that be possible?
I've got to declare a major, God.
Which really puts me on the spot.
All this thinking, praying, wondering—and no direct
    leading yet, Lord.
The only thing I have to go on is a growing interest in
    people.
I want to work with people, help them with their
    problems, alleviate their suffering, if I can.
Whether on the mission field, in counseling, in welfare
    work—that's what I want to do.
OK, so if I feel this way, I ought to major in social
    science.
Right, God?
I don't know what to do at this point, except step out.
On faith, so to speak.
Unless You give me a "Hold it!" feeling, I'm going to
    head that way.
So it's up to You, God.
Stop me if I'm wrong.

Summer's ahead, God.
Full of uncertainties for me this year.
I can't plan on working, I can't plan on school, I can't
    plan on anything.
Not till we get this lump business settled.
It's like there's a debate going on inside me.

Like, "Don't worry about that lump, Joel. It's nothing."
And, "But what if it's not 'nothing'? What if . . . . ?"
It's enough to tear a guy apart, God, this worry.
I know You say something about casting all my care
    upon You.
That's what I'm trying to do.
But there's this constant worry underneath it all.
I guess it's just because I'm human, right, God?
Well, at least I'll know about that lump pretty soon.
One way or the other.

Friday, June 2nd

Half-way through college, God!
Two years down, two to go.
I'll be through before I know it, and out into the cruel,
    cold world.
Look out, world!
Here comes Joel Stewart!

Saturday, June 10th

Well, God, You didn't answer me.
Not the way I hoped You would, anyway.
Dr. Johnson did *not* say, "It's nothing."
Instead, he looked serious—worried, even.
"I'd better do a biopsy," he says. "I'll take the node off
    the lymph gland and see what it is."
So it's all set.
I go into the hospital Thursday and have the node
    removed Friday.
I'm scared, but I realize it's the only thing to do.
At least, I'll know.
And that's better than wondering and worrying.

I wish I hadn't, God, but I did!

Looked up "lymph glands" and "nodes" and all that
    stuff in the encyclopedia.

God, You don't suppose I have cancer, do You?

There, I wrote it down.

The encyclopedia says not all such growths are malig-
    nant, but some are.

"Malignant" . . . "cancer". . .

God, I'm too young, I've too much of life ahead of me!

Don't let me have cancer!

Please, God!

Please!

I'm alone tonight, God.

In this hospital room.

Alone except for You, that is.

After Mom and Dad left, saying they'll be back in the
    morning . . . after supper (broth only) . . . after the
    nurse left . . .

I'm alone, with You.

I wish Mom and Dad were here, even if I am twenty
    years old.

I remember when I had the mumps, how, tossing all
    night half-delirious, I'd wake to find Mom and Dad
    sitting by my bed.

Quietly, calmly, patiently.

They'd touch my hot head, put cool cloths on it, pat my
    shoulder.

I wish they were here now.

I'm going to try to go to sleep, God, with a Bible verse
    vivid in my mind.

"Yea, though I walk through the valley of the shadow
   of death, I will fear no evil: for Thou art with me."
You've given me that verse, my special verse for this
   hard time.
I'm going to hold it tight—especially as I go into the
   operating room tomorrow.
"Thou art with me."
"Thou art with me."
Oh, God, I'm scared.
Scared.

Friday, June 16th

It's over, God, the operation's over.
I wasn't scared of the surgery: that I could face.
I was afraid of the results.
Here's how it happened, God.
I wake up early to find Dad and Mom coming into my
   room.
They squeeze my hand lovingly as we pray together.
Then I'm wheeled out and into the operating room.
Dad and Mom assure me they'll be waiting when I
   come back.
As I go spinning down the dark whirlpool, lights twirl-
   ing, falling, falling steadily into unconsciousness,
   Your voice comes to me, clear as anything.
"I am with you."
That means, I am in the "valley of the shadow of
   death."
But suddenly, I'm not afraid.
I'm reaching out for Your hand, which You are holding
   out, when everything blacks out.
Next I know, I'm trying to open my eyes, but they're
   heavy, weighted.
Everything's so far away.
I hear Dad's gentle voice: I guess he's seen me stirring.

"It's OK, son," he's saying. "Everything's OK."
God, You heard!
Thank You, thank You, thank You!
Thank You for making the node benign, not malignant.
Thank You for going with me through "the valley of the
 shadow of death."
My throat's sore; the small incision hurts; I'm limited
 to jello, soup, ice cream for the next few days.
But that's all nothing—compared to the fear that's
 been removed.
There's no cancer at all, God
No cancer at all.
Praise You!

Saturday, July 1st

Now what do I do, God?
I'm feeling fine: my throat's all healed.
And here's summer stretching before me.
With nothing to do.
Too late to take summer courses at junior college.
Dad's set me to work painting the house, for a fee.
That's great.
But I'd like something else to do, God.
Got any ideas?

Tuesday, July 11th

Another unexpected answer, God.
Almost before I asked.
Like, here comes Mr. Afton, the new church youth
 director.
I hardly know him: he's only been there since May.
Well, he stops by today, and there I'm perched atop
 the six-foot ladder, trying to paint the rafters under
 the eaves.

I put down the paintbrush and climb down.

I can't even shake his hand, mine's so gooked up with paint.

He's a really neat guy, God; I can see why the kids like him.

"Joel," he says, "I've come to ask you a favor."

My mind starts clicking: print the bulletin? substitute in a Sunday school class? or—perish the thought —paint the youth room?

He's going on, "Youth camp's coming up, you know."

Sure, I know, only I'm too old to go, I'm thinking.

"I'm looking for a counselor for the boys," he says. "Might you be interested?"

Me, I'm sizing up the situation, thinking fast.

And realizing that, after the house-painting job is done, there's nothing ahead.

But I'm a bit wary.

"What's involved?" I ask, trying not to be impertinent.

So he explains it's sort of "big brothering" the teenagers, playing ball, getting them to their Bible classes, keeping them quiet at night (oh, yeah? I remember youth camp dorms!)

And having devotions with them, counseling them spiritually.

There's a laugh for You.

Me, in need of spiritual uplift myself, counseling others?

Sort of "the blind leading the blind," I'd say.

Only something happens.

Excitement, peace, happiness?—something goes "click" in my mind.

Like, "Hey, Joel, maybe this is what God has for you this summer!"

Is it, God?

Is this Your will for me now?

It was, God, it was!

No doubt about it, this is what You wanted me to do.

How else could I explain this fantastic experience?

I've got as much out of it as the boys here—even more, perhaps.

Like, here in this nature-setting, woods, brook, hills and all, is one of Your temples.

It's rustic: only wooden benches, sawdust floor, open sides.

But You've been there, in the services, in the speakers, in the songs.

Like, there I sit in the choir, lifted up beyond words by the music.

Listening to You speak through those men You've chosen.

Hearing You say, "Joel, you're pretty special to me. I'm going to use you."

Like, how, God?

I'm waiting, eager, anxious to find out.

You've really got me, God—all of me.

I see now why this summer happened.

It's part of Your plan, to bring me close to You.

OK, God, here I am.

Send me!

4
Junior Year in College

Wednesday, September 6th

Its my junior year, God.
Funny how some lines I've heard stick with me, God.
"We live our lives in chapters," one speaker said.
Right, so here's "Chapter Junior Year at Stoddard"
    coming up!

Wednesday, September 13th

I've moved up, God.
To sports editor of the *Stoddard Standard*.
They said it was because of "qualifications and ex-
    perience."
I'll bet they couldn't find another willing goat.
It will be a lot of work.
But it will help with tuition costs.
Not bad, God.

Friday, September 15th

The Greeks said, "Know thyself."
OK, so I'm trying—to know me.
Like this barrage of junior tests: personality, achieve-
    ment, aptitude.
Wonder what they'll show?
At least, You know me—and You love me anyway.

God, meet Fred.

He's a junior college transfer, quite a card—a real character, in fact.

Already he's popular with everyone, including me: there's an intangible something that keeps us hanging around, wondering what's next.

Maybe it's because he's new and different: everyone else is "old hat."

Or because he's genuinely witty and clever.

Or because he says and does things we'd like to but don't dare.

Anyway, he's fun.

You'll probably be hearing more about him.

"Rich man, poor man, beggar man, thief,"

That's how I feel God; that's what the aptitude tests say.

"Journalist, social worker, CPA . . . "

CPA, *me?*

That's what Dr. M. says: I've an aptitude for figures.

(Not the curvy kind, but little numbers in books!)

Now, what am I supposed to do?

You've really got me, God.

I wish I knew.

Like I said, God, You're hearing more about Fred.

He's got a great idea, he says, like "Let's organize a union to get things changed around here."

"What things?" I ask.

"Oh, stupid rules, like No smoking, No drinking—we
    want the right to skip tests if we wish—no more
    grades . . . "
I gulp hard, thinking, "Look guy, if you're so hung up
    about rules, why did you come here in the first
    place?"
Only he doesn't give me time to say this: he's running
    along.
Something (Someone?) tells me Fred is bad news.
Should I stay away from him? help him?
Where does my responsibility lie, God?

Sunday, October 15th

Hey, philosophy's not bad, God!
Those old timers—Socrates, Plato, Aristotle—they
    really have some relevant things to say.
Maybe some of their thoughts will feed my thoughts.
Or help me understand myself, my problems.
What do You know!

Saturday, October 21st

I knew it; God—I saw it coming (or should have).
This Fred, he's really trouble.
Last night he shows up with an older, tough-looking
    guy.
And invites a bunch of us to his room to talk more
    about this "stand-up-for-your-rights" bit.
So we mosey in, half-curious, half-suspicious.
And this guy is lolling on the bed, lazily puffing smoke
    circles which smell "toasty," like grass.
(I know—I should have backed out then—but curiosity
        got me.)
So Fred and he pass knowing looks, and Fred starts in.

"Look, you guys," he sneers, "You're all cowards in this college, every one of you."

We tighten up, resentfully, as he probably knew we would.

Then he puts his joint out. "OK, show me that you're not. Here—" and he lights another grass roll and passes it to me.

Me, I sit there, staring at the smoke curling from its tip, wondering what I should do.

When he says, cynically, "C'mon, Stewart, show your guts."

I look sideways at the other guys; they're staring, fascinated, at me.

And somehow, something snaps, and I say to myself, "So what?" and pop the joint between my lips and take a deep drag.

Man, that smoke's smothering—it chokes me, makes my eyes water, sears my throat.

None of that calmness, that "high" I'd heard about.

As I'm sputtering, Fred and his cohort start roaring.

"Ho, ho, ho, Stewart," they guffaw; "Can't you take it?"

And they roll over, laughing, me all the while gasping, trying to get my breath.

All of a sudden, a big, guilty wave sweeps over me.

And something—Someone?—down inside of me says, "Joel Stewart! What *are* you doing?"

I'm so revolted by the whole scene that I feel like I've got to throw up, so I race out to the bathroom just in time.

And sit weakly on the edge of the tub, low in spirits, seeing how near I came to giving in and spoiling something very precious, my relationship to You.

Meanwhile, the rest of the gang, annoyed by Fred's attitude, troop out too, each feeling somewhat smutty over the whole affair.

What bothers me, God, is—I wanted to do it, to meet
    Fred's approval.
What is there in me that wanted to put him ahead of
    You? to defy You? to break Your laws?
I'm weak, God—I let You down.
But You didn't let me down, did You?
Thanks for bringing me to my senses.
And forgive me, God, please do!

Monday, October 23rd

Well, he's gone, God—Fred's gone.
Somehow the dorm director got wind of the ruckus
    and, about a half hour after we left, he and the dean
    show up in Fred's room.
And there are the two characters on the floor, both
    hyped on something stronger than grass, the nee-
    dles and powder lying right there on Fred's desk, the
    scars in their arms where they've been shooting it
    up for months (no wonder Fred always wore long
    sleeves).
So the police are called, and Fred and his friend are
    carted off to jail.
Just think, God, I could be there with them if things
    hadn't gone the way they did.
Thanks for keeping me from getting tangled into that
    mess.
Strengthen me to avoid temptation.
I wish I could have helped Fred, but he was beyond
    me.
He needs Your help now, God.
Please reach him somehow.

Thursday, October 26th

Life's a merry-go-round, God.

71

And me spinning madly in circles—like studies (four
    hard subjects)—sports editing (those Monday after-
    noon deadlines!)—track—the old landscape job.
How busy is "too busy"?
I think I'm that.

Sunday, October 29th

Life's a ferris wheel, God.
Not only going in circles, but up and down, too.
At youth camp I was on a spiritual high.
Now I'm on a spiritual low.
I've even missed church three Sundays, slept in, being
    tired.
What's wrong, God?

Saturday, November 18th

It just wasn't my day, God.
Track meet—and what do I do?
Come in fourth out of five in the 220, that's what.
I'm disappointed.

Tuesday, November 28th

Remember the redhead from Iowa, God?
That I wrote about last year?
She's in my Social Problems and Ethnology classes.
She's kinda cute.
Do You think she likes me?

Friday, December 15th

Sorry I haven't written, God.
It's the Post Office again, that's why.

Letters to right of me, letters to left of me, on the floor
   under me . . .
It's sheer nightmare!

Tuesday, January 2nd

Another beautiful Christmas home, God.
All the happy warmth of our childhood.
Plus the bonus of finding each other as new, grown-up
   people.
All three of us were home, God—plus Sarah, John's
   girl.
She's great, God—like the sister I've always dreamed
   of.
She and John seem so happy together.

Wednesday, January 3rd

Unbelievable! God.
Here are Jerry and Bob yesterday, healthy, happy, on
   their way back to Stoddard after vacation.
And today they're with You.
So suddenly!
Driving back at night, they were only forty miles from
   here.
And the predawn darkness (they've pegged it at 4:35
   a.m.), the car veers off the Interstate, skids fifty feet,
   hits the guardrail, becomes airborne off the over-
   pass.
And smash! it lands, upside down, on the ground sixty
   feet below.
What happened, God?
Why did Bob drift off to sleep (as he must have)?
Why didn't he wake up as he jolted off the roadbed?
Why did it happen at the overpass?

What went through their minds as they sailed off the
    road?
Did they have time to think?
How did it feel to crash-land like that?
Did they die instantly?
Or were they terribly hurt, to die painfully?
What's it like to go into Your presence, God?
Death seems, like, for old people, not for guys my age.
It makes me think, God.
It really does.

Wednesday, January 24th

Today I am a man, God.
In every legal sense of the word—twenty-one years
    old.
I know I haven't acted like a man this year—I've had a
    case of delayed adolescence, I guess.
I don't pretend to know everything.
But I do know I'm now fully responsible for myself.
What a burden that is!
Let's You-and-me carry it together, Lord, OK?

Monday, January 29th

Serendipity, God, that's the word to describe discov-
    ering this Bible verse.
I'm so sick of studying for exams.
And then I find a verse like "Of making of many books
    there is no end; and much study is a weariness of
    the flesh."
Amen, God, AMEN!

74

Know what, God?

I think Laurie (the redhead) likes me.

Which is a switch, since usually the girls I like don't get too excited about me.

Know how I know she likes me?

Well, I always study at this certain library table.

Lately, she's been at the same table, at the other end.

If she moves nearer my end, I'll take it as a sign.

And ask her for a date.

OK, God?

Missions Conference again, God.

Me, I'm as mixed up as ever: what *is* a "call"?

The messages, they hit me, down deep—but I don't want to mistake emotion or surface appeal for Your call.

Are You speaking to me?

Or am I hung up on the idea of being a noble, heroic missionary?

Here in my room, I'm not sure.

Sometimes I imagine myself as a missionary:

Flying into almost untouched tribal areas, bringing spiritual healing . . .

Standing under a tall palm at desert's edge, dark children clustering around me . . .

Going hut-to-hut to witness . . .

Going on safari . . .

Translating Your Word . . .

Teaching people to read it . . .

Then I take a good hard look at myself.

"What an imagination," I tell myself.

"Quit kidding yourself, Stewart," I say. "Missions is not glamorous: it's flies, dust, diseases, strange languages; it's a hard pallet at night; it's people turning away; even people spitting on you."
Could I take that?
I suppose I could if I were called.
But am I called?
That, dear God, is what I don't know.

Thursday, February 29th

Leap Year's Day, God!
And I "leaped"—right into a date with Laurie.
We were studying at the library, she right across from me at the table.
So I'm trying to make the outline for my Social Problems paper, and all I can think is, "She's there, Stewart. Ask her for a date."
She drops her pencil (on purpose maybe?) and it rolls under the table.
Sir Walter Raleigh Me, I dodge down under to get it—and there she is, bending down from her side, both of us grabbing for the pencil at the same time.
We look at each other, upside down, and start laughing.
Then we sit up and chat; talking to her comes naturally—it's even easy!
First thing, she's agreed to go to church with me Sunday night.
Fine, God, fine.
Only don't let me get stung again.

Monday, March 18th

This Laurie bit, God—it's going well.

Too well.

Dating in college is a whole different game from dating at home.

Like, instead of a once-a-week-plus-phone-calls thing, it's morning-noon-night right off the bat: church dates, meet for breakfast, study together.

Almost too much at once, God.

I think I like it—but I'm not sure.

Why does it have to be "steady" so fast?

Sunday, March 31st

Quite a twosome, God—that's us!

It's "Joel-and-Laurie" all over campus; everyone's pairing us off.

I like that, God—and I don't like it.

(Is this my old dual-me conflict rearing its ugly head? Or a warning from inside me?)

I like Laurie: we have lots in common, our dates are fun.

I can almost envision a future with her.

But I'm not ready for that, Lord.

I feel a little pushed.

Is there something wrong with me?

Thursday, April 4th

Back from my field trip, God.

Full of tumbling reactions.

Prof Kent (he teaches Social Problems), he's gung-ho for first-hand experiences.

So he sets it up with an inner-city mission for us to spend three days there, in the heart of the ghetto, in a broken-down, three-story brownstone building, just like the others in the block.

So we get "off-campus-activity" excuses from our other classes, pack our little satchels, and go "slumming."

Which we do in a skeptical, even ironical mood at first.

Which changes but fast, once we're there.

Talk about sensory impressions!

The sights: dirt, bleak walls, peeling paint, broken panes, filthy faces, smashed bottles, rotting oranges . . .

The smells: spaghetti-cabbage-beer-urine-filth-garbage all in one . . .

The sounds: toots, blares, beeps, sirens, loudspeakers, yells, screams, babbles . . .

It comes at us from all directions, constantly—no escaping it.

Reality hits us full force, no warning at all.

Well, we stay our three days, visiting the Salvation Army, the "Y," city welfare offices, food-stamp places, unemployment lines, adoption agencies, rescue missions.

Poverty . . . apathy . . . genuine need . . . lazy expectations—my feelings swing between pity for and disgust with the situation.

Why this reaction, God?

Is inner-city work for me?

Then why this simultaneous attraction and repulsion?

I'll tell You a secret, God—I was scared while there, really scared.

I wouldn't want to be on those streets alone, even in the daytime.

Of course, if You sent me, You'd be with me.

But I wouldn't go alone!

Friday, April 12th

Spring break coming up, God!

And two "biggies" on tap.
A track trip—three inter-collegiate meets and a regional in Des Moines.
Which, not being far from Laurie's home, leads to the second biggie: a visit with Laurie.
I'm eager to meet her folks, God.
But I'm nervous, too.
Who wouldn't be?

Monday, April 22nd

Two base hits, God!
The track trip went fine: Stoddard won one meet and placed second in the others.
And I won the 220 in regional!
Which was great, Laurie and her folks having come to watch me.
I was sure I'd fall flat, them sitting there and all.
But I didn't.
And when I felt that tape snap under my arms—Wow, God!
The gold medal is beautiful—I can't believe it's mine.
Thanks, God, for helping me do my best.
The visit with Laurie went fine, too.
They live on a farm in Iowa, acres of cornfields, rambling old house.
Todd (her kid brother, he's fourteen), is a character, a typical teen-ager.
Her Mom is warm and friendly, sort of like mine.
Her Dad's OK, too—a little brusque with me, perhaps?
(Maybe no guy is good enough for his little girl!)
It was great, seeing Laurie in her own background.
It was great, God.

Thursday, April 25th

Registration once more, God!

And for my senior year!
Since my major's settled, registration is pretty routine.
One course sounds exciting: Senior Practicum next
    spring, a try-out in various phases of social work.
I'm still looking for Your plan, God.
Don't forget, time is running out for me.

Wednesday, May 1st

What's the matter with me, God?
Everything's going great, just great, with Laurie.
She's bubbly over our relationship, looking to a future
    built on "Us."
And I get excited about it—when I'm with her.
Then, back in the dorm, I get panicky.
Like, am I ready to be tied down?
Then why do I long to be free, untrammeled, open to
    life's options?
Should I put on the brakes?
Have I led her along unthinkingly?
Am I just being childishly stubborn?
The old eat-your-cake-and-have-it-too syndrome?
Why can't I let go and become "serious"?
What's the matter?

Saturday, May 4th

Can't find a daisy, Lord.
Wish I could.
I'd not do "She loves me, she loves me not" with it.
Rather, I'd "I love her, I love her not."
Which is the Big Question right now.
Do I? or don't I?

Wednesday, May 15th

Hot-cold, Lord—me all over.

80

Sometimes I'm sure Laurie's for me and I'm for her.
Like tonight.
Coming back from the library, we sit by the fountain a while.
The lights play on the water, a rainbow spectrum breaks out—symbol of happiness.
She snuggles close, the breeze being chilly, my arm around her, her head nestled on my shoulder.
I kiss her.
We talk happily about "us," about being "engaged to be engaged."
And we part, happy, excited, hopeful.
Till I get to my room, and it hits me, full force.
What have I got myself in for?
Will I have to start planning ahead, seriously?
Am I ready to?

Sunday, May 26th

I've decided, God—I think.
I've got to be free this one more summer.
Free to work, to date if I want, to think things over, about me and Laurie.
Dad says, "When in doubt, don't."
So I'm asking Laurie to cool it.
Not to break up—no, God, not that!
We can be friends, very special friends.
We can write, phone, even visit each other.
But we must think objectively; we can't do that here at college, thrust together so constantly as we are.
We need the perspective of time and distance.
If our love lasts, it's real.
If it fades, it isn't.
It's the only thing I can do.
Help me tell Laurie, God, in the right way.

It wasn't easy, God, not at all.

Here we are, in a dim, quiet booth at Pete's.

A romantic setting—all too soon destroyed.

I lean across, to talk softly.

And her eyes light up with excitement, a deep brown glow.

But she notices the worry in my eyes, I guess—she pulls back slightly, still holding my hand.

"What's wrong, Joel?" she asks.

"Laurie," I say, courageously, "I'm worried. About us."

In those brown eyes there's a flicker of fear—it unnerves me.

"Look Laurie," I say. "I think I love you."

The flicker becomes hope.

"But I'm so uncertain of myself, Laurie. I can't trust my feelings," I say.

Then I explain to her what I wrote to You, like putting our relationship to the test, seeking Your leadership, wanting Your will.

(I'm not just dragging You in, God; You know that.)

Somehow, she understands.

I mean, she's disappointed, let-down, but sympathetic.

"Sure, Joel," she whispers. "We must make sure . . ."

There, in the privacy of the booth, we talk about how we can know Your will, and, holding hands across the table, pray right then and there, leaving it with You.

It sounds corny as I write it, God.

But it was a spiritual highlight.

God, if we're for each other, make our love grow stronger through separation.

If it doesn't, we'll take it as Your sign.

82

We're both trusting You.
We're open to Your leading, God.
We mean it—we really do.

He's done it, God!
John has got himself a wife—Sarah.
Me, I'm an usher, along with Jim.
There I stand, at the altar, watching them simply glow-
    ing as they take their vows.
They look deep into each other's eyes, with un-
    ashamed love.
And I feel a pang—a mixed pang—in my heart.
I miss Laurie so much I ache.
I wonder if I'll ever stand, as John is standing, as sure of
    my love for Laurie and hers for me, as John and
    Sarah seem to be.
God, bless them in their new life.
Bless Laurie and me, as we seek Your plan.
Bless us, God.

Sunday, June 9th

Tomorrow I'm going to work, God.
After dozens of letters, about ten applications, and two
    interviews—I've got a summer job.
Right here, in my own town, in the office furniture
    factory.
Pastor Rob helped a bit: he knows the personnel man.
So thank You, for working through Pastor Rob.
I begin tomorrow—night shift (they've got a big rush
    order on file cabinets).
My hands will be busy—but my mind free to think.
Just the kind of job I need.

Why didn't they tell me, God?
You know those little handles on steel file drawers?
Know how they get there?
They don't grow, that's for sure.
No, they're painfully screwed on by a pair of greasy,
    grubby, aching, blistered hands.
Mine.
Here's this conveyor belt going slowly by, bringing
    drawers.
Take screwdriver in hand—pick up two screws—pick
    up a handle—screw it on—shove the drawer along.
Drawer after drawer after drawer.
Like something out of *Fantasia*, a stream that won't
    stop.
I'm going bats, God.
Simply bats.

I'm tired, Lord, dog tired.
This job is really getting to me.
My hands are toughening up—my speed (I'm on
    piecework) improving.
But the monotony of it—and the hours!
10 p.m. till 6 a.m., all night long.
Drive home in the bright summer morning, eat,
    shower, hit the hay, out cold till suppertime.
Maybe see a ball game or a movie, back to work.
I simply can't get clean—grubby fingernails, greasy
    hair (Mom's making me use the same pillowcase all
    summer).
Only two redeeming factors:
    (1) My growing bank account, hopefully down
    payment for a car

(2) Laurie's letters, bless her.
They're frequent—they're regular—they're personal
   —they're sweet.
Just like her.

Friday, August 2nd

I'm worried, God.
Shouldn't be—it's what I offered Laurie.
But today's letter, in a sort of side remark, says, "Oh,
   remember Tom Terman from Stoddard? He's work-
   ing on a road crew here. I've been dating him a
   little."
Yes, I remember Tom.
And he can't have my Laurie.
My Laurie?
That's the way I feel.
But maybe she's changing her mind?
What have I let myself in for?
Four weeks to go, God!
How can I wait that long?

Friday, August 16th

Last night at the job, God.
Tomorrow our family sets out on a two-week trip to
   California.
Then back to Stoddard.
I wonder what I'll find?
How will Laurie feel?
How will I feel?
Her letters—they're wonderful—but that "bad word,"
   Tom, creeps into them.

I can hardly wait to see her—and I'm afraid to see her.
Same old dilemma, God.
Same old me.

5
Senior Year in College

What a let-down, God!
Bells and trumpets announcing my senior year?
Not on Your life!
First off, my stereo, carefully stored in the dorm
    basement—it's gone—swiped, stolen, ripped off.
I think I know who did it.
That gang Fred ran around with, they were in and out
    of here all the time.
And he worked for the Maintenance Department.
Maybe he got a key, had it copied . . .
I know, that's only circumstantial evidence.
But the stereo's gone—along with all my records, in-
    cluding my high school band and church choir
    ones.
Who'd want those?
Dad's household insurance covers the stereo—I can
    get another.
But those records, God.
I can't replace them.

Wednesday, September 4th

Another let-down God!
Here I'm waiting for Laurie at the student center, all
    tingly, 'cause I really love her.
She trips in, bubbly as usual, and I step forward, arms
    open.

Only to notice Tom waiting, too.
And she's looking at him, not me.
Big, handsome, brawny, tanned-from-his-summer-on-the-road-crew Tom.
Next to pale-face, hand-calloused, muscles-in-the-head-not-shoulders me.
I watch closely.
She doesn't rush to him—that's good.
She does light up inside—that's bad.
Me, I barge over with, "Hi, Laurie!"
She grins, that teasing grin, "Hi, Joel, how's every-thing?"
There we stand, Tinkers-to-Evers-to-Chance, Laurie-Tom-me.
She's friendly to us both, impartially.
Then it's, "Gotta go, guys . . . No, don't come with me . . . See you later!"
We're left there, staring—no, glaring at each other.
Until I shuffle off, leaving Tom to do likewise.
What gives, God?
What's happened?

Sunday, September 15th

What is it, God, a game?
Laurie seems to be playing Tom and me, both ends against the middle.
She'll study in the library with me . . . and have a coke with Tom.
She'll go to the game with me . . . and eat supper in the cafeteria with Tom.
I don't like it, God.
Not one bit.

We had the show-down, God.

It was inevitable.

I corner Laurie with, "I've simply got to talk with you."

"OK," she agrees happily, like we're on the same old comfortable footing.

So we walk through the pinegrove, like last year, and at our favorite spot I pause, bending to kiss her.

She pulls slightly away, with, "Don't, Joel, please."

"Why not?" I ask.

"I don't know why," she says bewildered.

"Is it gone, Laurie?" I ask, dreading the answer.

"I don't know, Joel. I just don't know," she says, tears in her eyes.

God, there's nothing makes me come unglued like a girl crying.

Maybe it's because I haven't had sisters, so I'm not used to it.

Anyhow, I take her into my arms, her snuggling comfy, like she belongs.

And I'm glowing with happiness.

Then she stiffens, pulling away.

"Please, Joel," she murmurs, "you've got to understand. I have to be free for a while."

"But I thought . . . ," I stutter, "this summer . . ."

"It didn't help one bit, Joel," she says. "It only mixed me up."

Then she explains how first she missed me so much she thought she'd die . . . then she got used to it . . . then Tom came along . . . they dated for company . . . then for fun.

And now she feels torn between us.

Well, it sounds dismal, so I drop my arms and step back.

I look at her little elfish face, screwed up in tears.

"OK, Laurie," I say gently, "if that's what you
    want . . . "
And I walk off, leaving her alone.
That was mean, God, I know.
But I couldn't stay, or I'd have blown it, letting her see
    my disappointment.
God, I'll have to let her go.
That was my bargain with You.
If her love has cooled, it has.
But why did mine grow stronger?
Why, Lord, *why*?

Sunday, September 22nd

If I weren't a senior, Lord, I'd cut out.
I'd go as far away as I could.
Why?
Because I can't stand seeing Tom and Laurie together.
Like they are all the time.
I should be big-hearted and say, God bless them.
But I can't.
Bless them if You want to, God.
But don't expect me to help.

Wednesday, October 2nd

Decisions, decisions, God.
Wrestling with them like the "multitudes in the valley
    of decision."
The same old questions.
What do You want me to do? and where?
(I'd like to ask, With whom? but I can't.)
Remember those aptitude-test suggestions last year?
I've eliminated CPA: too tedious, detailed.
And journalism: not enough professional training.

It's work-with-people, I guess God.
But what work? where?
You've really got me, God.
And time's running out.

Erase Laurie, God.
She's cut me cold—it's "Laurie-and-Tom" now.
I'm outside looking in, like a kid at a candy-store
    window.
I've gone through all the stages: hoping, wishing, de-
    spairing, hating.
Now I'm revengeful.
I'll show her, God, I sure will.
There's a new secretary in the business office, a cute
    blonde, right out of high school.
She's given me the come-on.
I'm going to make Laurie jealous.
Will that work?
Nothing ventured . . .

Great timing, God.
I ask Renee (the secretary) for a date and she says,
    "Sure, come on over to my apartment."
Apartment—*her*? She's only eighteen.
Anyhow, I get there and she's not ready.
"Just a minute, Joel," she tosses, peering out of her
    room, towel over shoulder, which towel she slips
    down, tantalizing-like, and disappears.
Her roommate, Barb, engages me in small talk, puffing
    lazy smoke circles.
Renee appears, in these slacks so tight you have to look

91

and this sweater that says, Wow.
So we go to the concert, and she's too cuddly, here on
our first date.
Then we head for Pete's.
I walk in, Renee hanging on, and there's Tom and
Laurie.
Laurie's face is a study, like she can't believe her eyes.
Good, old dependable Joel—how come he's going
out, not waiting in the wings for his call?
Soon she and Tom leave, her stealing a glance at us.
So I make sure my head's bent close to Renee's (which
takes courage, because of the cheap-perfume-
stale-smoke smell).
After I drop Renee off, I get to thinking.
I'm pleased—for "showing" Laurie.
I'm disgusted—at myself.
I don't think I'll see Renee again.
Once is enough.

Monday, October 21st

Once is enough, God?
Not for Renee.
She's after me constantly, by phone, with notes, chas-
ing me down the hall.
She has "problems," she says; she needs to talk with
someone.
I know it's a line, but I sort of fall for it.
So we've got a date to talk.
I feel stuck.

Tuesday, October 22nd

"Stuck," God?
Maybe so—but maybe I was supposed to be.

Renee sure needs help.
Here she is, only eighteen and she's tried every-
    thing—everything, God—smoking, drinking,
    marijuana, LSD, sex, the works.
Crazy mixed-up kid!
She says she respects me, that's why she's telling me.
Can I help her?
Under that paint, frizz, and dye, I see a pathetic little
    girl, needing You.
So I try to share spiritual ideas with her.
She says, here at Stoddard she sees something she
    hasn't got—You.
She says, she's through with the old ways.
Is this my work for this year, God—to help Renee?
Maybe . . . but I'm worried . . .

Wednesday, October 30th

Good ole "Uncle Joel," that's me, God.
Night after night, these "talk sessions."
Maybe they're helping: Renee does seem interested in
    the Bible, in You.
Maybe You're working through me.
I hope so.
Only, she takes so much for granted, like she thinks I'm
    hers.
She's so kitteny-cuddly, always rubbing up against me.
There's a reaction, God—I can't help it.
Is it affection I feel? love? or just the old sex urge?
I don't feel like I did (note past tense) about Laurie.
But I don't feel good about Renee.
Does she have to get her help from me?
I feel like I'm on quicksand.
Help me, Lord!

Now who's "crazy, mixed-up," God?

Me, that's who.

Like, objectively I tell myself, "Stewart, she's on the make for a man, any man. Get out while the getting's good."

So I brace myself to say that.

But she purrs, stroking my face, about how I've helped her.

And that old urge rears up, undermining my determination.

Then Laurie flits through my mind—only she's not "my Laurie" any more.

So I think, "Who cares?" and give in to Renee.

Oh, God, of course we don't play around: I know better than that.

But she's playing the "going steady" game, and I go along.

She's trapping me—and I'm letting her.

Why am I such a fool?

Out of desperation, because I can't have Laurie?

Out of "senior panic," wanting someone to belong to?

Out of rebellion, trying to run my own life?

Out of debt, really owing it to Renee to help her?

Why am I letting it happen?

I'm really in deep, God, over my head.

Like tonight, we're window-shopping (Renee's favorite game).

First thing, we're outside a jeweler's window, staring at engagement rings.

It being Thursday night, the stores are open.

"Let's pretend," she says. "The clerk will never know."

And she propels me in and there we are, at the counter, a tray of diamond rings before us, and the clerk's urging her to try some on.

Next thing I know, I'm signing for a $100 down payment, ten-months-plus-carrying-charges deal— $300 worth!

And walking out stunned.

Absolutely stunned.

Why didn't I put my foot down, God?

She's 1000 yards ahead of me in this race.

She's talking wedding—she's even set the date, May 30th.

Engagement? Wedding?

I don't think I've ever mentioned them.

How did it happen, God?

What happens now?

Saturday, November 30th

It's unbelievable, God.

The drama unfolds and I'm like watching myself go through it.

Here, I'm trying to quash Renee's enthusiasm.

But every time I try, she twists my arm.

I say, "Let's slow down a bit," and she pouts, "Why, Joel? Don't you love me?"

And the pout turns into a kiss-me pucker.

Which I, like a dope, respond to—and I'm sunk.

She's flashing the diamond all over campus—even where Laurie can see it.

And drawing up plans for an elaborate wedding, a show with her as Star.

I'm going down a maelstrom, God.

Is this the way a guy in love should feel?

It's irony, God, sheer irony.

Now that Renee's drawn the noose tight, Laurie's free.

I mean, she and Tom have broken up.

Here I go all-out to "show" her—and get "shown" myself.

Her roommate, Beth, bears the tidings: it's because of me Laurie's ditched Tom.

"How come?" I query, stupefied.

"Because when she saw Renee getting serious, she realized she's loved you all along."

Girls, God.

I'll never understand them.

Why didn't Laurie come out and say how she felt?

Why doesn't Renee buzz off?

Why don't I settle things?

When is this surrealistic drama going to end?

Change of pace, God.

Forget girls for a change.

It's back to the P.O. tomorrow, for three and a half hard weeks.

My goal this time: the rest of my car down payment.

(And to make up for the money down the drain on Renee.)

I'm going to start looking round at cars.

There it is, God—my car!

There, in the VW display lot, the one I've dreamed

about—a nifty little gold "bug"—black vinyl interior—"four on the floor" shift . . .

I've figured it all out, including costs, taxes, license, insurance, gas.

It's taking three jobs to pay for it: (1) the factory last summer, (2) the post office now; and (3) stocking shelves in the supermarket two nights a week, starting in January.

I'm all set, God.

I can hardly wait.

Thursday, December 12th

Dad's great, God.

On impulse, I phoned him—for advice.

Of course, I can buy it myself: I'm nearly twenty-two.

But I respect Dad's opinion.

He says it sounds great to him.

He doesn't know about the ring, though.

How can I tell him?

Saturday, December 14th

It's mine, God—all mine!

Mine and the Finance Company's, that is.

I can't believe the interest they charge: I'll be in hock for the next three years.

But it's worth it, God, every bit.

Driving out of the lot, behind the wheel of my own gold VW . . .

Rolling into the dorm parking lot, the other guys crowding around, admiring . . .

Taking Renee for a spin (and wishing it was Laurie) . . .

Putting the "bug" carefully "to bed" with a tarp over it
   tonight . . .
My very own car, God!
All mine!

Sunday, December 22nd

Got my fingers crossed, God.
About Christmas vacation.
Mom knows I'm interested in Renee.
And, bless her, she's invited Renee for Christmas.
Only we can't go for the whole week, she being tied up
   in her job and me behind in all my studies, needing
   to hit the library.
So we're driving down after work the 24th, coming
   back the 28th.
Not long—but long enough to see Renee in my setting.
Like John saw Sarah last year.
Maybe things will look clearer that way.

Thursday, January 2nd

It was a disaster, God, a real disaster.
We're not forty miles from here, Christmas packages
   and all, and she starts whining.
Like, "Why waste this vacation at home?"
And, "Why does your family have any claim on you?
   You're almost twenty-two."
And, "We ought to go somewhere together, just us."
So I pull over and park.
"Listen," I say firmly. "We're going home because I
   want to go. Because I've a family that's important to
   me. Because I want them to meet you."
(Sort of a love-me-love-my-family speech.)

"OK, Joel," she says, deadly sweetly. "Let's go."

I wonder at the quick change, but I'm too tired (dumb?) to think much of it.

Mom's a bit taken aback when she meets Renee, but very gracious.

Christmas Eve goes OK, and most of Christmas Day.

Then the nagging begins.

"Look, Joel, I'm marrying you, not your family."

And, "We've got to figure out how we can get some more money."

And—worst of all, "Hey, I know where we can sell that coin collection. It ought to pay for a swinging honeymoon."

Me, I shove that collection back into the safe deposit box but quick, before she can get her grubby, gold-digging mitts into it.

Teddy-dog, he avoids her, hiding out under the kitchen table.

Jim, he ignores her.

John, he's really teed off: he doesn't know it, but I overhear him and Sarah arguing about it in his room. He wants to tell Renee off, and Sarah says, "Don't; that will only make things worse," and "Joel will find out for himself."

So I'm glad when the 28th comes and we're back to Stoddard.

Only I can't buckle down to study.

God, how did I get myself into this?

I mean, I know *how* . . . I should ask, *Why*?

OK: (1) I wanted to hurt Laurie; I did.

     (2) I wanted to make my own decisions; I did.

     (3) I failed to consult You.

Well, it's not too late.

I know what I must do.

Somehow, I want to talk to Dad first . . . 'scuse me, God, while I phone him . . .

That was short, God—and not sweet.

Dad understands; he really does.

Only when I ask, "How do I get disengaged?" all he
  says is, "Just like you got engaged, Son. Start talking."

OK, I'll start.

But how? where? when?

Whew, it's over, God.

And I'm sure glad.

I call Renee, "How's about cruising around town?"

She agrees, always being ready to go.

When we park, I don't take her in my arms.

Instead I look her straight in the eye

"Renee," I blurt out, "I've made a terrible mistake."

"Like what?" she asks, teasing.

"I'm serious," I go on. "I want to break our engagement."

Her face is a study—God, if only I could have recorded
  the expressions.

Surprise . . . disbelief . . . cynicism . . . hope . . . despair . . . disdain . . . hatred flit past.

She fumes and fusses, rants and rages, swears and calls
  me everything in the book.

Then come the gallons of tears and the recriminations.

And the demand that I drive her home.

Which I do.

She storms out of the car, ripping off the ring and
  flinging it in my face.

Me, I'm sitting there aghast.

I hadn't expected the melodramatics, I guess.

When she's gone in, I put my hands over my ears to

100

drown out the vicious sounds.

I lay my head down on the steering wheel to catch my breath—and pray a bit.

The ring, there on the carpeting, glints coldly, and I pocket it.

Suddenly I realize I'm wet from perspiration—and cold.

I drive slowly back to the dorm.

Spent, emotionally drained.

But free, God.

Free!

Friday, January 10th

I've lucked out, God.

That jeweler—he's not a bad guy at all.

Like, today I take the ring back, fearful, anxious.

He's not surprised: maybe this happens oftener than I thought.

He adjusts his Cyclops eye and peers at the stone steadily, turning it this way and that.

"Pretty good shape, boy," he says. "She must have taken good care of it."

"Will you take it back?" I ask, humbly.

He peers again, a long minute, then nods.

"Of course, you'll have to take a loss," he says.

OK, that's only fair—I forfeit the $100 down and two months' payments.

An expensive lesson, God.

But well learned.

Sunday, January 12th

Sorry, God—my one-track mind.

In all this Renee business, I forgot to mention.

Pastor Rob talked to me when I was home—about
being assistant director at the youth camp this
summer.
I'd like to—it will all depend on what I do when I
graduate.
If I have to begin on a job right away, that's out.
If not—it might be right for me.
Wouldn't it, God?

Friday, January 24th

What a hassle it's been, God.
Books, term papers, exams, reports—is there no end to
the academic pressure?
Considering everything, I haven't done bad this semes-
ter.
Just one more to go—and still so many unanswered
questions.
Are there any answers, God?
I'm beginning to wonder.
You've really got me, God!

Wednesday, January 29th

Now, about fire, God.
You'd think, being once burnt, I'd stay away from fire.
But not when it's there, burning steadily underneath all
the while.
After Renee, I get my head cleared and start thinking.
It dawns on me: I'm ready for love, real love.
So, after my last exam, I roam into the student lounge.
Laurie's there, flipping idly through a magazine.
I wander over to the newspapers, pretending to be
interested, all the while with half an eye on Laurie.

Then I say, "Joel, stop playing coy. Get with it."

So I go right over and sit down beside Laurie.

She looks up, not especially surprised, and grins, "Hi, Joel."

I take the magazine, set it down on the coffee table, to have her full attention.

"Laurie," I begin, my stomach full of butterflies, "I've got to talk with you."

She raises her eyebrows slightly, like in "Oh?"

"Laurie," I say, "I've been an utter fool. What I've done is unforgivable, but can you forgive me?"

She faces me directly: "What's with Renee?" she asks, mincing no words.

So I say, "Let's go riding, and I'll tell you."

So there we are, cruising along, and I'm pouring out the whole sordid mess to her, not trying to exonerate myself, just explaining.

She relaxes visibly, takes a deep breath, and starts explaining the Tom episode.

There we sit, counselor-counselee, playing both roles at once.

Somehow, suddenly the whole burden is lifted.

From both of us, apparently.

She reaches out timidly, and at the touch of her hand—it all comes back to me.

And she whispers, "Joel, I've always loved you."

And we melt into each other's arms, crying and happiness all rolled together.

All those wasted months, God!

And the happiness now!

I want to jump, sing, shout Hallelujah!

Laurie loves me and I love her.

I can't believe it!

Joy, joy, joy!

There's a golden glow, God.
Over everything I do.
Mostly because I'm back right with You.
And back right with Laurie—my Laurie.
My problems—they're less, now that they're shared.
My joys—they're doubled, also because they're shared.
Thank You, God, for keeping me from a total mistake . . . for renewing my contact with Laurie . . . for bringing us back together.
Somehow, we know this is Your plan.
Thank You, God, thank You!

Monday, February 10th

Remember Senior Practicum, God?
I wrote You about it last spring.
We've had to sign up for three types of work, out of a possible six or eight.
My choices are (1) welfare, (2) boys' home, (3) "Y."
OK, I've started the ball rolling.
Now, You direct its course, will You?
I start the 18th, in the welfare office in Cantor City, under a Stoddard grad who works there.
I was turned off by inner-city work last year.
But I'm testing that reaction.
I want to be—I must be—open to anything You want.
Show me Your plan, God, through this practicum.

Friday, February 14th

Valentine's day, God.
A very special day, now that I've found my true love.
There's no doubt about it, God.
No doubt.

104

Welfare worker #24730 reporting, God!

Finished my Cantor City welfare practicum yesterday.

I still feel mixed reactions.

The first week, there I am in the office, sitting by the interviewer.

The cases that came in—You wouldn't believe them, God.

Poverty etched in deep-lined faces, despair, discouragement, humiliation.

Mothers toting smelly babies, toddlers hanging onto dress hems.

Shuffling old men, bored-looking young ones.

Could I be an interviewer, ask the right questions, make the right decisions?

Could I tell the needy people from the con-men, the worthy from the unworthy?

The second week, it's with the field worker, investigating homes.

Rat-trap tenements . . . dingy, filthy stairways . . . garbage . . . and battered doors . . . sleazy, crowded, noisy, reeking apartments . . .

It turned my stomach, God, literally.

That's not living; it's just existing.

Could I be an interviewer or a case worker?

I wonder, God.

What a great practicum, God!

I'm assigned to Bryson Ranch, the denominational boys' home.

First week, I'm a general "flunky" there, assigned to a cottage Dad.

I help some of the boys repaint the kitchen, bring in the cattle for milking, visit their school, play tag football, show them some track pointers, sleep in their rooms.

The second week, I'm in the office, pounding a typewriter, writing up case histories, answering the phone, interviewing two new guys who've arrived (their mother is dead, and their father deserted them), working up adoption papers for a young couple.

You know how newly-hatched ducklings tag after the first moving object they see?

Well, there's this little guy, about six years old, who tags along after me like that.

Guess he's in need of "big brothering."

One night, two of the older guys and I sit up late, by the crackling fire, after the younger kids are tucked in.

Just hacking around, talking, the way we do at youth camp.

I think it helped them to confide in someone my age.

What a tremendous two weeks this has been.

Is this for me?

Saturday, March 29th

Why the "Y," God? (Pun!)

Another two-week internship, split between office and recreation duties.

The first week, general detail—and a chance to speak at the local Rotary about the practicum.

The second week, deep into PE: morning jogs, noontime slimdowns for tired middle-aged men, after-school basketball, evening swims—a real workout!

The director seemed pleased—even hinting about a job when I graduate.

I said I'd think about it, so I'm thinking.

OK, this is the way it lines up now:
   (1) Welfare work—no thanks.
   (2) Boys' home—really great.
   (3) "Y" activities—so-so.
Where do I go from here?
So I've talked it over with Laurie.
We've decided I should write for jobs, maybe in the
   "Y" field, definitely in the boys' homes area.
Show me how to get going, God.

Monday, March 31st

Well, that was a speedy answer, God!
This morning in practicum review, Prof Peavy comes
   in with a handful of papers.
Which he flicks through, saying they're job possibilities.
Which we can, if we wish, look through.
And we do, avidly.
I see they fall into three categories, more or less.
   (1) Those requiring only a B.S., like I'll be getting in a
   few weeks.
   (2) Those requiring a master's, which I maybe ought
   to consider getting.
   (3) Those asking only a B.S. now, but will ask for
   more, perhaps even subsidizing a master's program.
I've picked out fifteen that look interesting, from all
   three categories.
Also found four more, through the college employ-
   ment office.
That gives us (Laurie and me) nineteen—no, twenty-
   one possibilities.
Tomorrow I'm going to write.
The extra two are grad schools, just in case.
Prof Peavy said I could use him as a reference.

(Guess the practicum went OK, then!)
I'll talk these over with Laurie; we can compose a sample letter together.
Hey, I'm supposed to be meeting her now.
Gotta run, God.

Wednesday, April 2nd

See my great map, God?
Adds color and glamor to an otherwise drab wall.
Also keeps me posted on job progress!
There are 21 blue thumbtacks, one for each place I've written.
All the way from Michigan to Texas, Wyoming to Georgia.
See, we're open to any place You want to send us—*any* place.
If a letter comes back, "No thanks, kid," I'll change the blue tack for a red one ("Stop!").
If it says, "Perhaps," yellow ("Maybe") goes in.
If it's promising, there'll be a green ("Go").
See, here are the thumbtacks—red, yellow, green.
You decide what goes where, please, God?

Friday, April 4

Spring break coming up, Lord.
And I'm taking a last fling, so to speak—and Laurie understands.
I'm driving Bert and Jeff to Florida, to see Jeff's uncle.
But mainly I'm going to have a week in sunshine, surf, and sand.
A sort of bon voyage to boyhood.
I'm really looking forward to it.

You wouldn't believe it, God.

But it really happened.

We arrive at Jeff's uncle's house late Saturday, after hours of driving.

Tired, we sack out in sleeping bags on his sun porch.

Sunday, we go to church and hike along the white sand hunting seashells.

(I keep wishing I could share all this with Laurie—I miss her so much.)

Monday I decide to take the bus to Daytona, where the action is.

Fearing I'll be "rolled," I hide my watch and wallet in my suitcase, taking only enough cash for rides and food.

Monday's a blast there; I decide to stay overnight.

Only, low on funds, I settle down in the bus station to wait the night out.

I'm dozing there on the hard bench when I'm rudely shaken awake by a rough hand.

And a rough voice, "Get up, you lug. What do you think you're doing?"

It's a local cop , one of Florida's "best."

I try to explain, but I start stuttering.

He takes a good look at the old Army jacket I'm wearing (the one I got for a buck fifty at the surplus store), thinking I'm a drifter, and demands some I.D.

I reach for my wallet, only to remember it's back in my suitcase.

I try to explain again, but he gets huffy and hustles me to the patrol car.

When I was a kid, I always wanted to ride in a police car, but not this way.

At the local court, they book me on vagrancy.

They're marching me toward the cells when I remember my rights.

"How about a phone call?" I insist.

They grudgingly OK it, so I phone Dad, but fast.

Now, it's about 1:30 a.m. home, and Dad answers, half asleep.

"I'm in jail, Dad," I tell him, and he snaps awake.

Now, I'm no kid running crying to my father: it's just that I need advice.

"What can I do to help, son?" he asks.

"Talk to the cop," I plead, handing the officer the phone.

Dad assures him I'm not a runaway and I am a responsible citizen.

He also suggests I phone Jeff's uncle, which the cop reluctantly agrees to.

By now, it's like 4 a.m. in Florida.

But Jeff's uncle is great: he decides to let me cool off in the clink the rest of the night, but promises to be there—with my wallet—when court opens.

I'm ushered into a small, dark cell, crowded with three other men: a sullen long-haired guy, a toothless drunk, and a fat man snoring on one of the bunks.

I crawl into my corner, lying down fully dressed, ignoring my cell-mates.

I drift in and out of nightmarish sleep, wondering how this all happened.

What I've done is not wrong, but it *is* dumb, I'll admit.

I ask Your help in getting me through the ordeal.

Breakfast comes at 6:30—sloppy cereal, a dry, hard bun, coffee.

I'm hardly presentable for court, the wrinkled Army fatigue jacket, stubbly chin, towsled hair.

Pretty soon, court opens, and I'm taken to the room, to be stared at by unsympathetic faces, yawning clerks, curious customers.

I look around; there's Jeff's uncle in the doorway, with

my suitcase in hand.

I could hug him, I'm so glad to see him . . . but I don't.

I retrieve my wallet—with that valuable ID—from my bag.

And turn to face the judge, grateful that Jeff's uncle is right beside me.

The judge reads the charges, scowling at me over his half-glasses.

"What do you have to say?" he asks, curtly.

I explain briefly, showing him my ID, which he examines closely.

Then he turns to Jeff's uncle; "Is he with you?"

Jeff's uncle, bless him, accepts responsibility for dilapidated, unshaven me.

The judge ponders.

"OK, I'll release you into this man's custody. No record on this. But don't get picked up again, and get out of Daytona as fast as you can."

He doesn't have to tell me that, I'm already scrambling into Jeff's uncle's car.

And we're riding back to his home, him giving me some advice on general appearance and manly responsibility.

Which I take humbly, after all he's done for me.

I sit on his sun porch and try to sort the whole thing out.

Why did this happen?

And, how do I tell Laurie?

And, what lesson is there for me?

There always is, I know, Lord!

Maybe this will help someone else some day?

Monday, April 14th

Back with Laurie, God.

Where I belong!

111

She was great—even though I was embarrassed to tell
  her, she understood.
That's the best part: when you love somebody, you
  love them no matter what.
My mailbox was stuffed—seven letters (one from
  home).
OK, four red thumbtacks, one yellow, one green (from
  the ''Y'' secretary for northern Kansas, wanting
  more information).
Would I like that work?
If You want me to have it, I would.
It's up to You, God.

Tuesday, April 19th

Going home for the weekend, God.
It's a long pull for a short stay, but we're cutting
  Friday's and Monday's classes (don't tell the dean!)
It's that important to me, really.
I want to see Laurie in my home, with my folks.
We need this one more test.
Guide us, God.

Wednesday, April 23rd

She really belongs, God!
The minute we stepped in the door, it seemed like
  Laurie was part of the family.
Mom and Dad loved her.
So did old Teddy-dog, who trailed her every step.
We went to all my favorite spots . . . looked at family
  albums . . . met some of the relatives . . . saw some
  of the gang.
And came back tired, happy, and assured!
We do belong, God.
We really do!

112

Forgot to mention it, God.

When we were home, Pastor Rob asked me again about youth camp.

I'd love to do it—but how does that fit into Your timetable?

I've got to know pretty soon, God.

The deadline is May 30th.

Should I take it now?

If so, what if a job opened up then, to start June 1?

You've got to manipulate the timing, God.

It's up to You.

Saturday, May 3rd

Countdown, God—four and holding.

Four weeks, that is, till graduation.

Eleven red tacks, three yellow, five greens to date . . . and two I never heard from.

I'm following up on the greens—transcripts, references and all.

I even have an interview set up, with the "Y" representative.

I'm letting You take charge, God.

"Anywhere with Jesus" we'll be glad to go.

(Notice I said "we"?)

Sunday, May 4th

Meet Mrs.-Joel-Stewart-to-be, God.

Here we stand, hand in hand, my Laurie and I.

We've settled it . . . we've promised each other our lives, our love.

The future is good.

Especially since it's in Your hands.
Talk about mercy, God—we don't deserve such happiness.
And abundance—"above all that we ask or think."
We praise You, God.

Tuesday, May 20th

A real "red-letter" day, God!
I can hardly believe it; it's all coming through at once.
First there's a letter in the mailbox from graduate school.
I'm accepted to start in September . . . I'm even encouraged to apply for a research fellowship . . . it's a two-year program, work-and-study.
Hey, OK, I think to myself, and head for the phone to call Laurie.
The phone's ringing as I approach, so I answer it.
And it's for me.
It's the director of Bryson Ranch, the boys' home where I did the practicum.
He says, warmly, "Hello, Joel. What are you doing after graduation?"
Right to the point, just like that, no shilly-shallying.
Me, I stumble, "I'm not really sure, Mr. Dodson. I just got accepted at Cromwell University for work toward an M.S. in Social Work."
To my surprise, he booms, "Great! That fits perfectly!"
My silence must have confused him, because he says, "Are you still there, Joel?"
"Yes, sir," I answer.
"Well, I've got a proposition to make," he says. "Listen . . ."
And he explains the home has just been funded for an experimental apprenticeship-study program, a three-year deal, in which a guy will live and work at

Bryson (part-time sports director and counselor) and study at Cromwell part-time.

"Would you be interested?" he asks.

Would I be interested?

I stand there stunned, receiver in hand, the pieces falling into place like a jigsaw puzzle starting to go together right.

I'd really loved Bryson, I loved every minute of it.

But there weren't any job openings then, none I could fit into, anyway.

Now this way, I can be both earning and learning at the same time.

Maybe Laurie and I can get married this summer.

Laurie loves little kids too . . . she'd adore living at Bryson.

Like . . . lots of things.

Meanwhile, Mr. Dodson, he's on the other end, waiting.

He says, "Joel? Joel, are you still there?"

Then he says he's coming in to Stoddard Thursday, and will I think about it, and will I meet him for coffee to talk it over, and he hopes I'll really consider it, because he thinks I'll fit their "team" . . .

Well, God, it happened just like that.

I'm leaning against the wall, utterly unbelieving.

And right then and there, praise wells up from my heart to You.

It sounds so *right*!

I phone Laurie, and she's exuberant.

And we meet and rejoice together.

The details are so exciting.

Here's my acceptance at Cromwell already in hand when this Bryson offer comes . . . like, in Your word, " . . . before they call, I will answer" . . .

And here's my growing interest in Bryson, in the boys there . . .

Is this the way You guide, God?
By circumstance and growing interest?
I think it is.

The interview's over, God.

It went just great.

Like there we sit, Mr. Dodson and I, over coffee in the
    student lounge.

Just like co-workers, which we soon will be.

The interview isn't what I'd expected, all questions-
    and-answers.

Instead, Mr. Dodson starts talking about a couple of
    problem boys . . . or, as he calls them, boys with
    problems

One of them I remembered, one who sat by the fire that
    night, talking.

"I hope you'll keep touch with that boy," Mr. Dodson
    says. "He really respects you."

We keep talking, about other boys, plans for sports
    activities, and so on.

First thing, Mr. Dodson's standing, starting to leave.

"Haven't you some questions, Mr. Dodson?" I ask.

"Not really, Joel," he smiles. "I checked you out pretty
    thoroughly before I made the offer. Have you?"

Well, no, I really haven't, having got a letter from him
    about job specifications, study plans, salary, hous-
    ing, tuition allowances.

So we shake hands on the deal, him saying, "I'll have a
    contract in the mail tomorrow."

Then, just as he's leaving, he turns and says. "How
    about bringing Laurie out to Bryson Saturday to
    look the place over?"

Which is fine with her, so we're going.

116

This will be the last sign we'll ask, God.
Help us to sense Your will as we feel it out.
If we both feel Bryson's right, that will be it.
OK, God?

It's right, God, it's right!

Rolling across the prairies, through the wide old stone gate, up the tree-lined drive . . .

Seeing the bungalows nestled comfortably, the red barns, the trim gardens . . .

Meeting the boys again (and some of them remembered me, especially Little Duck) . . .

Meeting the staff again, the slaps on the back, "Glad you're joining us, Joel!"

Laurie loves it here too.

We spent about an hour with Mr. Dodson, working out some last details.

What about housing? (a small sports-director's cottage, sometimes with one or two especially hungry-for-love boys as "guests").

When does it begin? (September 1st; hope you can find something to do this summer).

Etc., etc., etc.

OK, God, we believe You've answered.

"Praise God from Whom all blessings flow . . . "

That's "our song," God . . . it truly is!

Sunday, May 25th

Wrote a letter today, God.

To Pastor Rob, accepting the youth camp assistant directorship.

The timing's perfect, isn't it?

Here I'll be doing that during July and the first two weeks of August.

Then I'll have two weeks . . . two weeks for Laurie and Joel.

Then start at Bryson the 1st of September and Cromwell the 15th.

More jigsaw puzzle pieces—the picture's almost complete.

Did you know the picture from the beginning, God?

You sure did.

Now You're unfolding it to us.

We like what we see, God.

It's a beautiful picture—of Your love.

Wednesday, May 28th

Shopping day, God—for rings.

Not like that last horrible, "grabby" experience . . .

Not the same store, either, You can be sure!

In a simple beautiful little store, an older, fatherly man waited on us.

Showing Laurie some tasteful, lovely-but-not-extravagant rings.

Just like Laurie herself!

We chose a diamond, a single, elegant diamond, sort of smallish, but perfect, in a dignified yellow-gold setting.

We also had a pair of wedding rings put back on lay-away for later on.

I tucked the ring into my pocket, and we drove to the pond just beyond campus.

There, with the soft breeze rippling the water and ruffling Laurie's hair, the warm sunshine reflecting our love, I took her hand and carefully, gently slipped the ring on.

And kissed her, right there and then . . . a slow, soft, promising kiss.

Which she returned.

God, I love her so!

We've set the date—August 23, a week after I finish at youth camp, with a week for a honeymoon before moving to Bryson.

At times I almost have to pinch myself.

Is this all true?

Or an exquisite dream from which there'll be a rude awakening?

Then I touch Laurie, and it's no dream.

I reread my contract with Bryson, and it's no dream.

I look over my acceptance at Cromwell, and it's no dream.

It's for real, God.

For real!

Friday, May 30th

Graduation tomorrow, God.

For both Laurie and me.

Six months ago, before I found out Your plan, I dreaded graduation.

Tonight there's regret, even nostalgia, at this exciting chapter in life coming to a close.

But there's excitement and anticipation for the future.

My future—our future—Your future, God!

"The lines are fallen unto me [us] in pleasant places," God.

We accept Your will.

With joy.